Daodejing

The *Daodejing* is the most fundamental scripture of Daoism and a classic of world literature, as important to human culture as the Bible, the Quran, and the dialogues of Plato. It is at once a repository of ancient wisdom, a key to understanding present-day Chinese civilization and culture, and a source of astonishingly fresh perspectives on hot social topics and existential issues. In the *Daodejing* one finds discourses on life, death, sex, and human emotions, as well as war, capital punishment, and effective leadership.

Although traditionally ascribed to one author called Laozi, the *Daodejing* is really an ancient "hypertext," with inputs from many hands over several centuries. It is profound and many-layered, but its poetic imagery, proverbs, riddles, and aphorisms converge on the central theme of *wu wei* or noninterference. *Wu wei* is based on the idea that active intervention causes more problems than it solves. The *Daodejing* preaches the virtue of noninterference and letting things evolve naturally. In personal life, it recommends avoiding physical and mental friction, preserving one's energies, and staying healthy. In government, it warns against activist policies that waste resources and ultimately strengthen rivals. The human world and its social order are a natural part of the cosmos. Allowing events to unfold naturally is always better than striving and forcing change.

The *Daodejing*'s philosophical themes are revealed most fully in its imagery. The root, the wheel, the valley, water, and other metaphorical images recur frequently and are keys to unlocking its meaning.

Daodejing

(*Laozi*)

A Complete Translation and Commentary

by

Hans-Georg Moeller

OPEN COURT

Chicago and La Salle, Illinois

Publisher's Note on Names

Daodejing is the up-to-date name for the text traditionally known as *Tao Te Ching*. The titles *Daodejing* and *Tao Te Ching* are different representations of the same title arising from different romanization systems. The title *Tao Te Ching* was transliterated from Chinese using the older system, known as Wade-Giles, which dates back to the 1800s. The title *Daodejing* represents the newer romanization based on the pinyin system, which was introduced in the 1950s. Pinyin was officially adopted by the People's Republic of China in 1979 and is now used by most publications and libraries in the Western world as well.

At one time, the author of the *Daodejing* was thought to be a person named Laozi (Lao Tzu). Thought many scholars now dispute that the text has a historical author, it is still often referred to as "the *Laozi*" or "the *Lao Tzu*."

To order books from Open Court, call 1-800-815-2280 or visit www.opencourtbooks.com.

Open Court Publishing Company is a division of Carus Publishing Company.

© 2007 by Carus Publishing Company

First printing 2007

Printed and bound in the United States of America.

Library of Congress Cataloging-in-Publication Data

Moeller, Hans-Georg, 1964-
    Daodejing (Laozi) / complete translation and commentary by Hans-Georg Moeller.
        p. cm.
    Includes bibliographical references and index.
    ISBN-13: 978-0-8126-9625-7 (alk. paper)
    ISBN-10: 0-8126-9625-5 (alk. paper)
  1. Laozi. Dao de jing. I. Laozi. Dao de jing. English. II. Title.
    BL1900.L35M62 2007
    299.5'1482–dc22

                                                    2007016228

Contents

Preface

This English translation of the *Daodejing* is based on my German translation of the Mawangdui silk manuscripts version (unearthed in 1973 and dating back to circa 200 BCE). The German translation[1] was published more than a decade ago, but my basic approach to the text has not significantly changed since then. I still read the *Daodejing* as a philosophical text, and I think that its primary subject is order and efficacy within society and, by extension, within the cosmos. I also still think that the text, despite its cryptic nature, makes sense as a whole. My commentaries on each chapter—which have been more or less completely rewritten and reformulated—are meant to expose the meaning of the text and to present it as a coherent philosophical work.

The *Daodejing* is not an easy text to read, translate, and interpret. Still, I believe that if we distance ourselves a bit from contemporary reading habits and from what we expect of a philosophical text, we can soon gain an insight into its structure and sense. If only read closely enough, the imagery of the text provides access to its meaning. The images of the wheel, the gate, the root, water, and so forth, set up a network of semantic cross-references. They are the linguistic "links" within this ancient Chinese "hypertext" that lead from one verse and chapter to others. In a way, the *Daodejing* is highly repetitive. It is all about the workings of the "Dao," a scenario of perfect functioning in all realms of the world, be it the body, society, or nature. Images, metaphorical expressions, and symbols occur and reoccur through-out the text and refer to the same structures and maxims, such as the relation of emptiness and fullness or "presence" and "nonpresence" (*you* and *wu* in Chinese), as well as to the strategy of *wu wei*, or, liter-ally, "nonaction." I hope that this translation and its commentaries may help readers find their way through the captivating poetical and philosophical web of the *Daodejing*.

---

1. *Laotse: Tao Te King; nach den Seidentexten von Mawangdui* (Frankfurt/Main: Fischer, 1994).

As for the original text, I have to admit that this translation is not based on a single version of the *Laozi*. Given the number of existing versions—of which none can claim to be "the" original—it would be completely arbitrary to declare that one of them is the "definitive" and then ignore all others. The *Daodejing* evolved over a long period of time, probably from oral sources, and there is neither an identifiable author nor a standard version. Following the likes of Hall and Ames (see below), I have tried to identify a reading that made good sense by making best use of the various philological materials at hand. For a more detailed discussion of the history of the text and my understanding of its genesis I refer the reader to the introduction and appendix.

Although the main sources for my German translation were the Mawangdui manuscripts, for this edition I have also considered the Guodian manuscripts as well as a host of other early editions that are collected in Shima Kunio's *Rōshi kōsei* (Tokyo, 1973). I have given special attention to the commentaries and/or editions ascribed to Heshang Gong and Wang Bi. In my comments, I sometimes refer to the version or commentary to which that specific translation relates. I have also consulted a number of modern Chinese editions and commentaries to the text, including Chen Guying's *Laozi zhu yi ji pinglie* (Peking, 1984), Huang Zhao's *Boshu Laozi jiaozhu xi* (Taibei, 1991), Jiang Xichang's *Laozi jiaogu* (Shanghai, 1937), Ma Xulun's *Laozi jiagu* (Peking, 1956), Xu Fancheng's *Laozi yijie* (Peking, 1988), Xu Kangsheng's *Boshu Laozi zhu yi ji yanjiu* (Hangzhou, 1985), Yan Yiping's *Boshu zhujian* (Taibei, 1976), Yan Lingfeng's *Mawangdui boshu Laozi shi tan* (Taibei, 1976), Zhang Songru's *Laozi jiaodu* (Jilin, 1981) and Zhou Ciji's *Laozi kaoshu* (Taibei, 1984).

Several English translations and commentaries have been consulted as well, particularly Roger T. Ames and David Hall, *Dao De Jing: "Making this Life Significant"; A Philosophical Translation* (New York: Ballantine, 2003), Wing-tsit Chan, *The Way of Lao Tzu* (Indianapolis: Bobbs-Merrill, 1963), D. C. Lau, *Chinese Classics: Tao Te Ching* (Hong Kong, 1982), Robert G. Henricks, *Lao-Tzu: Te-Tao Ching; A New Translation Based on the Recently Discovered Ma-Wang-Tui Manuscripts* (New York: Ballantine, 1989) and, by the same author, *Lao Tzu's Tao Te Ching: A Translation of the Startling New Documents Found at Guodian* (New York: Columbia University Press, 2000).

I have chosen not to translate the term "Dao." Perhaps its most important meaning is "way," but in the context of Daoist philosophy, and Chinese culture in general, it has taken on a much broader significance. Since the term has found its way into other languages, including English (one may think of phrases or titles such as "The Tao of . . . "), I decided to leave it at that. I did, however, translate the nearly equally important Chinese term "De." Common English translations for this word are "power" and "virtue" (for instance, in the sense of "by virtue of" which connects to the meaning of "power"). I settled on the somewhat more uncommon and certainly less pleasing term "efficacy" since I think that it renders the meaning of the Chinese term more adequately. In my commentaries I also speak of the sage and, particularly, the sage ruler as "he." I chose the male and not the female or neutral form on purpose. In the historical context of the *Daodejing*, rulership was, however unfairly, associated with men.

As in previous cases I am greatly thankful to Ryan O'Neill for mending my English and to Cindy Pineo at Open Court for all the work she did to improve the initial manuscript.

—Cedar Bay, Friday the 13th, January 2006

Introduction: Of Whirls and Wheels

In a study on the Daoist "classic" *Zhuangzi*, the German sinologist Hans Peter Hoffmann discusses two intriguing articles that might help to shed some light on the origins of the imagery and philosophy of the *Daodejing*.[1] The first of these articles is by the contemporary Chinese scholar Pang Pu[2] and presents a hypothesis about the genesis and cosmological background of the term *xuan* ("dark") that figures so prominently in the *Daodejing*. One of its most important appearances is at the end of the first chapter. Here it is stated in relation to the Dao: "Darker even than darkness—Gate of multiple subtleties." Pang tries to reconstruct why the term *xuan* combines the three meanings of "dark," "mysterious," and "cosmic essence." He suggests that the Chinese character for *xuan*, as it appears in its earliest form on oracle bones, depicts two hands that turn something around and around creating the motion of a whirl: 𢆶. A whirl, Pang concludes, is deep and *dark*, and can be associated with the *mysterious* downward spiraling of water—with a black hole of water, so to speak. The whirl functions as a gate that lets all things in and out like a *cosmic source* through which everything passes. He then refers to a set of objects from a late-stone-age culture named Qujialing that were unearthed in 1955 in the southern Chinese province of Hunan and initially interpreted as a type of ancient spinning reels (Fig. 1). Given the number, color, and the peculiar design of these objects, Pang doubts that they were used simply as spinning tools and instead suggests that they were ritual objects. He assumes that a bamboo stick was put through their empty hub, that they were then spun and, when they turned quickly, their design looked like a whirl in the shape of the letter "S"—very much like the ancient form of the character *xuan*. The notion of

1. Hans Peter Hoffmann, *Die Welt als Wendung: Zu einer literarischen Lektüre des Wahren Buches vom südlichen Blütenland (Zhuangzi)* (Wiesbaden: Harrassowitz, 2001), 187–206.

2. Pang Pu, "Tan 'xuan,'" in *Yi fen wei san: Zhongguo chuantong sixiang kaoshi* (Shenzhen: Haitian, 1995), 284–94.

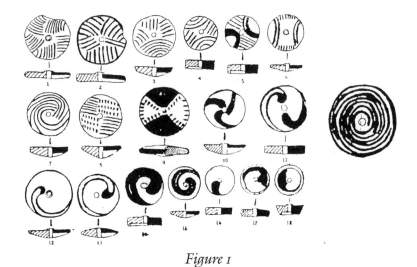

Figure 1

xuan can thus be associated with the motion of such a turning wheel, which again can be associated with the functioning of a "dark" and "mysterious" cosmic gate. Pang Pu relates this set of imagery, rightly I believe, to the imagery of the *Daodejing*.

The second article referred to by Hoffmann is an archaeological study by the French scholar Alain Thote on a coffin and some related objects excavated in 1978 from a tomb at Leigudun in the province of Hubei.[3] The Leigudun tomb was dated to circa 433 BCE. Thote states: "Many bronze fittings or bronze vessels discovered at Leigudun are ornamented with the whirl motive."[4] The ornamentation of these objects bears a clear resemblance to the "spinning reels" discussed by Pang Pu (Fig. 2).

Interestingly enough, Thote also mentions another prominent set of images found on the inner coffin of the Leigudun tomb: "The main subjects of the lacquer paintings seem to be the openings—whether doors or windows—and the hybrid creatures which stand beside the openings, in an apparently protective position."[5] These are images of the windows and doors with and without the "protection" of some half man–half animal beings shown by Thote (Fig. 3).

---

3. Alain Thote, "The Double Coffin of Leigudun Tomb No. 1: Iconographic Sources and Related Problems," in *New Perspectives on Chu Culture During the Eastern Zhou Period*, ed. Thomas Lawton (Princeton: Smithsonian Institution/Princeton University Press, 1991), 23–46.

4. Ibid., 29.

5. Ibid, 35.

Figure 2

Figure 3

As Pang Pu does, Thote thus, at least indirectly, relates the imagery of a whirl to the imagery of openings or gates ("doors or windows").

The Leigudun finds are associated with the culture of the southern Chinese region and the state of Chu. The Qujialing culture predates that of Chu, but it existed within the geographical reach of what later became Chu. The *Daodejing* is also associated with the Chu culture, and ancient Daoism is believed to have developed or at least to have had a "stronghold" there.

The chapter in the *Daodejing* that is for me the key to its imagery and philosophy is chapter 11. It begins:

> Thirty spokes are united in one hub.
>> It is in its [space of] emptiness,
>> where the usefulness of the cart is.
> Clay is heated and a pot is made.
>> It is in its [space of] emptiness,
>> where the usefulness of the pot is.
> Doors and windows are chiseled out.
>> It is in its [spaces of] emptiness,
>> where the usefulness of a room is.

The image of the wheel, consisting of the hub and the revolving spokes, is, as I have repeatedly claimed in my interpretations of Daoism,[6] a structural blueprint for the relation between a central emptiness (*wu*) and a peripheral fullness (*you*) that turns around it and thus results in a revolving motion which represents the Dao. If one looks at the "spinning reels" of Qujialing and the whirl motifs of Leigudun, and if one takes into account that these were obviously prominent elements in rituals and, by extension, expressions of the cosmological imagery in the region of what became the state of Chu, then it leads one to see some sort of connection or development from the imagery of Qujialing to the artifacts of Chu culture and finally to the poetry of the *Daodejing*.

It is quite interesting to note that the first stanza of chapter 11 in the *Daodejing* not only introduces the image of the wheel but also

---

6. See my *Daoism Explained: From the Dream of the Butterfly to the Fishnet Allegory* (Chicago: Open Court, 2004), 27–36; and *The Philosophy of the Daodejing* (New York: Columbia University Press, 2006).

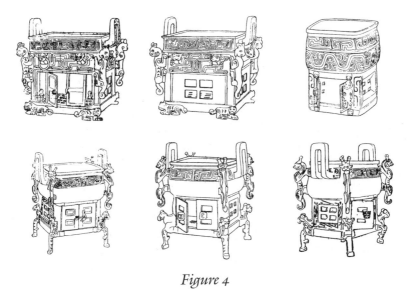

Figure 4

the images of the pot, or the container, and the doors and windows. The motif of "openings" or "windows" is, as suggested by Thote, the main subject of the lacquer paintings on the coffin of Leigudun, and, as to the bronze containers, they are "shaped like a room and are fitted with doors and windows."[7] Here is what these bronze vessels look like (Fig. 4).

Chapter 11 thus seems to connect with a more ancient imagery used particularly in the region of Chu: not only to wheels, reels, or whirls turning around an empty hub, but also to vessels, containers or pots, and, last but not least, to rooms with doors and windows. The motif of the whirl, as connected by Pang Pu with the character *xuan*, could have had the significance of a cosmological "gate" through which all things must pass—through which everything enters and leaves the present. This interpretation would fit with the context of the whirls and openings found on the Leigudun artifacts. After all, these were burial objects and thus immediately related to the coming in and, particularly, the going out of the world.

The *Daodejing* is replete with images that can be associated with the imagery from Qujialing and Leigudun. The wheel or whirl, doors, windows, and gates, "darkness," an emptiness surrounded by fullness, revolving or returning motion (as in chapter 40: "Reversal

7. Thote, "Double Coffin," 35.

is the movement of the Dao"), the "going out into life, going in into death" (chapter 50) — all this seems to belong to a complex of imagery that evolved in the region of Chu or that at least played an important ritualistic and cosmological role there. I would dare to speculate that the imagery used in the *Daodejing* has its roots in this complex of imagery. Given the long historical interval between the late stone age, Chu culture, and the first known "complete" form of the *Daodejing* (the Mawangdui manuscripts that date back to around 200 BCE), one has to be very cautious when determining the meaning or the ritualistic function of these images and objects. I would certainly refrain from claiming that the ritualistic meaning of the whirling "spinning reels" of Qujialing is to be equated with the meaning of the first lines of chapter 11 in the *Daodejing*. Still, it seems to be a reasonable hypothesis that the imagery used in the *Daodejing* evolved from certain origins. Given the evidence of archeological finds in the region of Chu and the association of the *Daodejing* with Chu culture, it also seems reasonable to assume that the cosmological and ritualistic motifs of Chu had some influence on the poetic imagery of the *Daodejing*.

Given the archaeological evidence, I would go as far as to speculate that the *Daodejing* "secularized" the ritualistic and cosmological imagery of Chu and transformed it into a philosophical imagery that expressed a political vision of social order and a cosmology of the Dao. The *Daodejing*, as I read it, is a political and "meta-political" text (in contrast with the "meta-physics" of ancient Greek philosophy). It probably relied on a long history of "sacred" imagery and transformed these into philosophical poetry. In my brief commentaries on the individual chapters of the *Daodejing* I attempt to elucidate in detail the philosophical meaning that this imagery took on.

Daodejing

Text and Commentary

One

一

As to a Dao—
> if it can be specified as a Dao,
> it is not a permanent Dao.

As to a name—
> if it can be specified as a name,
> it is not a permanent name.

Having no name
> is the beginning of the ten thousand things.

Having a name
> is the mother of the ten thousand things.

Thus,
to be permanently without desires
> in order to see the subtleties.

to permanently have desires
> in order to see that which is yearned for.

The two—
> together they come to the fore,
> differently they are named.

Together they are called:
Darker even than darkness—
Gate of multiple subtleties.

Commentary on Chapter One

In his *Philosophical Investigations*, Ludwig Wittgenstein discusses an image that can be seen as a duck or, conversely, a rabbit.[1] Wittgenstein calls the switch from seeing the duck to seeing the rabbit a "change  of aspect." I believe that the first chapter of the *Daodejing*, and particularly its first stanza, is also based on a "change of aspect." The first two sentences (As to a Dao—if it can be specified as a Dao, it is not a permanent Dao / As to a name—if it can be specified as a name, it is not a permanent name) are linguistically parallel, just as the lines used for drawing the duck or the rabbit are essentially the same. We can, however, interpret the same structure differently and reverse, so to speak, the front and the back.[2]

The Dao is understood by the Daoists as something permanent. Particularly in the *Daodejing*, permanence (*chang* or *heng* in Chinese) is often enough associated with the ideal scenario: the perfect "way" (*dao*) functions constantly and is not subject to cessation. Thus, judging from the philosophical context, we can be quite sure about at least one aspect of the meaning of the first sentence: The Dao is something that is permanent. Insofar, however, as the Dao is a perfect scenario, a "way" that goes on smoothly and interruptedly, it is also a way that includes opposites. Day and night (the way of time) and the four seasons (the way of the year) are scenarios that go on permanently. But the going on of these temporal processes is not reducible to one of their specific aspects. The way incorporates opposites. If we want to

---

1. Ludwig Wittgenstein, *Philosophische Untersuchungen* (Frankfurt/Main: Suhrkamp, 1984), 520.

2. The only contemporary Western interpretation known to me that interprets the relation between the first two sentences in the way of an aspect change is presented by Herlee G. Creel in his article "On the Opening Words of the *Lao-Tzu*," *Journal of Chinese Philosophy* 10 (1983): 299–329.

grasp a Dao in its permanence, we cannot specify it. It is, as a whole, not something specific. To specify it would mean to miss it.

The following sentence is structured in parallel. Its meaning, however (as I believe), is reversed—just like the orientation of the head(s) of the rabbit and the duck. A name, as opposed to a Dao, does not designate something permanent. "Day" and "night" are the specific components of the course or way of time—they are specific and can be named with specific names. Every Dao, which itself is not specific but permanent, consists of specific elements that can be given specific names but are not permanent. The specific components constitute a nonspecific whole. The meaning of the first stanza thus is (in my interpretation):

A Dao cannot be specified—and thus is or can be permanent. Names, conversely, specify things and are thus themselves specific. This is why they cannot designate that which is permanent. Names designate the specific segments that constitute the permanent Dao. There is a shift of aspects between the Dao and the names. They relate to each other just like the duck and the rabbit in Wittgenstein's image.

The following two stanzas about the respective having and not-having of names and about the having and not having of desires may be read similarly. With respect to the whole of things, there is a change of aspects between having and not having (of names and desires, etc.). *Wu* ("not-having") and *you* ("having"), or, as I prefer to translate these terms when standing on their own, "nonpresence" and "presence," are the two integrated aspects of the functioning of the world. They function in combination. The Dao "as such" is nonpresent (and without a name or desires), but it is the "beginning" and inclusive of all that is present (and has names and desires). The Dao that has no name (or the sage ruler who manifests it in the human world and who has no desires) integrates that which has specific names (or, in the state, the people who have specific desires). Ultimately, the Dao and the specific elements that constitute it are one, but we need to perform a shift of aspects to see them as such. Thus, although the two aspects come to the fore at once, in combination they are rather tricky or "dark," and quite subtle. The concluding images of darkness (see, for instance, chapters 6, 15, and 56), subtlety (see chapters 15 and 27), and the gate (see chapters 6, 20, 52, and 56) are quite common images of the Dao.

5

Commentary on Chapter Two

This chapter continues the main theme of the preceding chapter—the permanence of the impermanent. The course of time, the extension of space, and even our judgments come in corresponding pairs. Both temporally and spatially a before goes along with an after; and if one introduces categories such as good and beautiful one also implies their opposites. While none of these aspects is permanent on its own, they are permanent in conjunction. Before and after change and cease to be, but the change between before and after is incessant. In society, the specific evaluations of good and bad vary, but they thereby constitute an ongoing process of evaluation.

The sage marks the position of the Dao in this ongoing process or discourse, namely, the nonpresent in the midst of the present. The sage takes on no specific duty and does not take part in the discourse about the good, the beautiful, and the ugly. However, this passivity on behalf of the sage is for the sake of the activity that surrounds him. It is exactly because of his passivity that the actions in the realm of the people and in nature can go on. The nonpresence of the Dao and the sage are not antagonistically opposed to presence, but they nevertheless are, like the empty hub at the center of the "full" spokes (see chapter 11), the necessary pivot around which all activities circle and which thereby constitutes the unity and harmonious balance of the whole scenario.

There are two kinds of complementary oppositions. First, there is the opposition between the segments of change (before/after, good/bad, and so forth). Second, there is the opposition between this very realm of change (as constituted by the oppositions just mentioned) and the empty pivot of change. The sage (ruler) and the Dao manifest the pivot. They are permanent and without presence, action, or speech within the realm of continuous change, action, and speech.

Two

二

Everybody in the world knows the beautiful as being
    beautiful.
        Thus there is already ugliness.
Everybody knows what is good.
        Thus there is that which is not good.

That
        presence and nonpresence generate each other,
        difficult and easy complement each other,
        long and short give each other shape,
        above and below fill each other,
        tones and voices harmonize with each other,
        before and after follow each other,
is permanent.

Therefore the sage
        resides with the task of nonaction,
        practices the teaching of nonspeaking.

The ten thousand things—
        he makes them work, but does not initiate them,
        he makes them act, but does not depend on them,
        he makes them complete their tasks and does not reside
           with them.

Well,
        only because he does not reside with them,
        they do not depart.

7

Commentary on Chapter Three

This is a rather straightforward chapter. It was Confucian doctrine to promote the worthy in order to have the most virtuous people in the government. From a Daoist perspective such a practice will only lead to conflict among the people. They will develop a desire for political powers that creates a competitive atmosphere, which poisons social harmony. Similarly, the display of scarce luxury goods will unnecessarily and artificially create needs. Obviously, Daoists cherished neither political competition nor an economy based on demand. Politically and economically, they envisioned a state of contentment rather than one of contention. The chapter advises the sage ruler, on the one hand, to provide for basic needs, particularly for sufficient food, and, on the other hand, to prevent any kind of craving for more than is needed. Satiation and satisfaction are reached when a mindset of yearning is avoided. If such a mindset cannot be avoided, this will lead to a state of addiction and strife. The people's desire for consumption would be awakened and there would be a permanent struggle among all.

Interestingly enough, the yearning that the Daoist sage ruler is supposed to prevent explicitly includes the desire for intellectual "properties" such as knowledge. Addiction is not limited to material goods and social power. Just as material indulgence may lead to a state of a continuous want for more and better goods, intellectual indulgence might create a hunger for more understanding or information. Peace of mind among the people—and a peaceful society—can only be attained if the arising of both physical and mental yearnings is quelled.

Three

≡

When the worthies are not promoted,
    then this will make the people not contend.
When the goods that are difficult to obtain are not esteemed,
    then this will make the people not become robbers.
When that which is desirable is not displayed,
    then this will make the people not disorderly.

Therefore the ordering of the sage is such:
    He empties their hearts;
    he fills their bellies.
    He weakens their wishes;
    he strengthens their bones.

Persistently he makes the people have no knowledge and no
    desires.
He makes the one who knows not daring, not acting—and
    this is all.
    Then there will be nothing that is not ordered.

Commentary on Chapter Four

The first line of this chapter presents one of the core aspects of the Dao: It is empty, and its emptiness cannot be used up. Like a gate (for this image of the Dao see, for instance, chapter 1 and chapter 6) it does not lose its efficacy when used. Because it is imperishable in its usage it resembles the "ancestor of the ten thousand things" or the "divine ancestors." As a perennial gate, it brings forth without tiring. Like water it is an incessant source of nourishment. There is nothing that precedes it—nobody knows whose child it is.

One should, however, still be more than cautious in interpreting the Dao as a transcendent origin. It is a constant source of fertility, like a root or water. But as a source it is not "ontologically" separated from that which it originates. It is empty, like a door. This means that it is still in the midst of the process of generation. In Chinese ancestral religion the divine ancestors were likewise thought to still exist. They were the nonpresent, but not absent, source of the clan. One had to feed them and one could, through divination, communicate with them. That the Dao is compared to a divine ancestor does not mean that it is essentially separated from the realm of presence. It does not belong to another world, a world detached from ours. Like the empty space within a door it has to be there for us to go in and out—it is the nonpresent at the heart of the present.

The middle stanza reappears slightly altered in chapter 56. It seems to describe the leveling effect the Dao has over time. That which is sharp will be ground down, and so on. The Dao, once more, functions like water. In the course of time it smoothes the sharp edges and evens out the uneven.

Four

四

The Dao is empty,
      and when it is made use of, it still does not become full.
What an abyss!
It resembles the ancestor of the ten thousand things.

Grinding the sharp,
      loosening the tangled.
Dimming the shine,
      leveling the dust.

How deep!
      And seemingly there.
I do not know whose child it is.
It resembles a forbear of the divine ancestors.

Commentary on Chapter Five

This is one of the most outspoken nonhumanist chapters in the *Laozi*. Just as heaven and earth (or nature) do not treat the "ten thousand things," that is, all the kinds of beings in the world, with compassion, so the sage does not have particularly humane feelings for others. Still, this does not mean that the sage despises humankind. He is totally unbiased and impartial—and void of one-sided emotions. To the sage there is simply the Dao as a process of change, and it is "unwise" to be emotionally attached to particular elements within this process at the expense of others.

The chapter may also be interpreted as a criticism of ritualistic Confucianism. Traditionally, straw dogs were used as ritual objects and highly revered. But when the ceremony was over they were trampled upon or burnt in the fireplace.[3] Thus, even such respected objects were eventually disregarded. This contradictory practice is mocked in this chapter. The Confucians celebrate in their rituals (particularly in those connected with funerals and ancestor worship) the continuity of the clan; they revere the dead as if they continued to live. Ritual integrates the deceased into the world of the living. But the treatment of the straw dogs demonstrates that a ritual ceremony cannot really grant permanence to things or people. Once the ceremony is over, the ritual objects are once again "dead." The Daoist sage does not cling to rituals that are supposed to grant permanence but are themselves obviously subject to change. The sage knows, just as nature, that human beings, just as the ten thousand things, will perish within the course of change. Humans are not an exception. They are as much a part

---

3. This practice is described in the *Zhuangzi*; see the *Zhuzi jicheng* edition of the *Zhuangzi jishi* (Peking: Zhonghua: 1954), 99–100, and A. C. Graham's translation: *Chuang Tzu: The Inner Chapters* (Indianapolis: Hackett, 2001), 82. There is an alternative reading of this passage that interprets the last two characters not as meaning "straw dogs," but as "straw *and* dogs." This interpretation goes back to Wang Bi's commentary. I, however, follow the reading of Wing-tsit Chan, *The Way of Lao Tzu* (Indianapolis: Bobbs-Merrill, 1963), 107, and many others.

of the course of Dao—which is a process of change—as anything else.

The second stanza introduces the image of the bellows. This image is parallel to the images of the wheel, the door, or the valley in that it depicts a structure that is empty at the center and full in the periphery. Due to this structure, the bellows can function incessantly—its emptiness can never be used up, and so it is of ongoing use. While individual things (such as straw dogs and humans) are impermanent, processual structures of emptiness/fullness can function without exhaustion.

The final stanza compares the "commonsense" understanding of wisdom and rulership with a Daoist strategy. Ordinarily one would say that listening a great deal to what goes on and thoroughly investigating affairs would be beneficial for ruling. From a Daoist perspective, however, to "hold on to the center" is more effective. The sage has to stay calm at the center of society just as the hub stays unmoved at the center of the wheel. By being inactive and not interfering the sage provides for the unity of society.

Five

五

Heaven and earth are not humane.
>They regard the ten thousand things as straw dogs.

The sage is not humane.
>He regards all the people as straw dogs.

The space between heaven and earth—
>Does it not resemble a bellows?

Empty, but not consumed,
>The more it is moved, the more comes out.

Hearing a lot, investigating much—
>this is not as good as holding on to the center.

Commentary on Chapter Six

This chapter combines a number of important Daoist images: the valley (see chapters 28 and 39), the gate (see chapters 1 and 10), the feminine (see chapters 10, 28, and 61), and the root (see chapters 16, 26, 39, and 59). The valley and the gate are, like the bellows and the wheel, Daoist images of the emptiness/fullness (or nonpresence/presence) structure. The valley, the female, and the root are also images of inexhaustible fertility. This chapter makes it clear that the Dao is a way of generation and (re-)production. The "spirit of the valley" expresses the Dao's function as a permanent source of life (and death).

Six

六

The spirit of the valley does not die—
    This is called: dark femininity.
The gate of dark femininity—
    This is called: root of heaven and earth.

How ongoing!
    As if it were existent.
    In its use inexhaustible.

Commentary on Chapter Seven

Heaven and earth constitute nature, and nature is an enduring process. The sun, the moon, and the stars circulate constantly as do the seasons. The earth gives new life every year—and human life in an agricultural society depends on this selfless quality of the earth. Nature does not know selfishness. The course of nature, the Dao, is without purpose or intention. It is exactly this purposelessness and lack of self-interest that the Daoists associate with permanence or, rather, the permanence of change. Only such a nonattachment, particularly to oneself, allows for the steady course of change to go on unimpeded. The sage models himself after the selflessness of nature and thus develops a paradoxical strategy. Because he has the least possible self-interest he qualifies as the leader of humankind. No one is as qualified as him for integrating humankind into the selfless but steady course of nature. His lack of ambition and personal purposes establishes him as the ruler. This is his peculiar negative self-interest. By eliminating all selfishness he realizes his potential as ruler. His aim is reached when he has reduced his ambitions to zero.

Seven

七

Heaven is enduring;
the earth is long-lasting.
The reason why heaven and earth
     can be enduring and long-lasting
     is that they do not live for themselves.
Therefore they can live enduringly.

Therefore the sage
takes back his own person,
     and will personally be in the front,
keeps his own person out
     and will personally be established.
Is this not because he has no self-interest?
Thus he can bring his self-interest to completion.

Commentary on Chapter Eight

Here, the Daoist sage ruler is depicted through the use of the image of water. Water benefits (and nourishes) everything that grows on earth because it takes on the lowest position. The Daoist sage is supposed to rule likewise. In paradoxical Daoist fashion, the one who withdraws and does not struggle—as the previous chapter stated it—is the best qualified for being the ruler. It is obvious in this chapter that the Daoist sage as "the best" is also intended to be the political ruler. The second stanza explicitly talks about "ruling" (*zheng*) and taking care of affairs (*shi*). To be trustworthy in speech and giving are cherished qualities in a regent. It is noteworthy that the chapter also mentions another quality of a ruler: to make his subjects perform actions at the right time. Such timeliness was of great importance in a society that was dependent on agriculture and thus on work that was in line with the course of the year. The ruler had to issue the calendar and initiate the respective phases in the yearly cycle of life and work. Timeliness in harmony with nature was also vital in public works and in warfare. These activities could only be fruitful if things were done (or not done) at the right time.

It is not clear from the text if the second stanza speaks literally about the Daoist sage ruler (here I have chosen to read it in this way by inserting a "he" at the beginning of each sentence) or of the working of the Dao. But this is not really decisive. In any case, the Daoist sage ruler is supposed to rule in accordance with the Dao. He is supposed to rule in society with the same timeliness and order as the Dao "rules" in nature.

Eight

八

The best is like water.
    The goodness of water consists in
    its being beneficial to the ten thousand things,
    and in that it, when there is contention, takes on
      the place
    that the mass of the people detest.

Thus [the best] is close to the Dao.
His position
    is good in placement.
His heart
    is good in depth.
His giving
    is good in nature.
His speaking
    is good in trustworthiness.
His ruling
    is good in ordering.
His taking care of affairs
    is good in ability.
His having actions performed
    is good in timeliness.

Well,
    it is because only he does not struggle
    that there are no calamities.

Commentary on Chapter Nine

From a Daoist perspective the accumulation of goods and wealth will, paradoxically, lead to loss and perhaps disaster. The advice is therefore not to hoard things. Similarly, it is not beneficial to "sharpen" one's tools. That which is too sharp is prone to break. This is certainly meant allegorically. If one tends to create conflicts and is eager to contend, one will squander one's energies and soon be exhausted. The displaying of wealth, strength, and a willingness to fight will unavoidably lead to tension and possibly one's downfall. The Daoist sage follows the opposite strategy and withdraws. He does so to be in line with the working of the Dao, the empty center that remains hidden behind the productive process nourished by it.

Nine

九

To pile it up and to fill it
     is not as good as ending it.
By forging and sharpening it
     you cannot keep it for long.
A room full of gold and jade—
     no one can guard it.
To be esteemed, wealthy, and proud,
     is to draw misfortune onto oneself.

To withdraw oneself when the work proceeds—
     this is the Dao of heaven.

Commentary on Chapter Ten

Apparently, the first three sentences of the first stanza discuss methods of bodily cultivation—an indicator of the presence of such practices in early Daoism. What exactly these techniques consisted in is difficult to say. It is interesting to note, though, that the image of the infant is mentioned. Here, as in other chapters (20, 28, 55) the sage tries to emulate the infant. This state, one can infer, is free of self-consciousness, completely spontaneous, and without intentions. Such Daoist practices as "nourishing the soul" and "embracing unity" may well have been used to reach an infantlike state. The following lines are more political in nature. Obviously, bodily cultivation was taken to be an integral part of being a sage ruler. The intertwining of bodily cultivation and the art of rulership is also present in early Confucianism and chapters 13 and 54 in the *Daodejing* also allude to it. The images of the gate and of femininity that occur in the fifth sentence connect this chapter with chapter 6. The sage ruler rules on the basis of feminine qualities and, presumably, holds on to the position of the empty gate in the "opening and closing" of the reproductive course of nature. The second stanza connects to this imagery of fecundity and of giving life. As is the case with the bellows (see chapter 6) the sage is able to continuously produce and "to let things out" without ever being thereby exhausted.

Ten

$+$

When you nourish the soul and embrace unity,
      can you stay undivided?
When you concentrate the Qi and attain softness,
      can you be like an infant?
When you cultivate and clean the dark mirror,
      can you become flawless?
When you love the people and revive the state,
      can you stay without knowledge?
When heaven's gate opens and closes,
      can you be the female?
When bright clarity extends over the four directions,
      can you stay without knowledge?

To give birth to it, to rear it,
to give birth to it without possessing it,
to let it grow without commanding it,
this is called: dark efficacy.

Commentary on Chapter Eleven

For me, this is one of the most important chapters in the *Daodejing*. It combines the images of the wheel, the pot, and the room (or the window, and, by extension, the door), and it connects these images explicitly with the relation between the empty and the full or nonpresence and presence (*wu* and *you*). Moreover, these images are also portrayed as images of functionality. They represent perfectly structured "scenarios" that obviously stand for the Dao and are thus capable of utmost efficacy (*de*). Thus the chapter sums up the teaching of *dao* and *de* in a nutshell. The structure of an empty center and a full periphery functions not only "materially" or "mechanically" but also "spiritually" or "mentally." The sage is supposed to empty his mind to bring himself in order, and the sage ruler at the center of society is empty of action and thus allows the state to function well. It is important to note that in all cases emptiness or nonpresence goes along with presence and fullness. Emptiness alone is not enough and does not "exist" for its own sake. A center needs a periphery to be a center. Daoism is not one-sidedly focused on emptiness or nothingness. It is only one (but literally the central) aspect of the Dao that cannot be isolated. Together emptiness and fullness bring about benefit and perfect use.

Eleven

十 一

Thirty spokes are united in one hub.
      It is in its [space of] emptiness,
        where the usefulness of the cart is.
Clay is heated and a pot is made.
      It is in its [space of] emptiness,
        where the usefulness of the pot is.
Doors and windows are chiseled out.
      It is in its [spaces of] emptiness,
        where the usefulness of a room is.

Thus,
      there is presence [*you*] for the benefit,
      there is nonpresence [*wu*] for the use.

Commentary on Chapter Twelve

From a Daoist perspective, one has to be cautious when it comes to the senses. However, I do not think that this chapter is ascetic in character. The spectrum of colors, tones, and tastes (the "five colors," and so forth) are not to be avoided completely. The problem is that in overindulging in them, one loses the capacity to enjoy them. When, for instance, one eats spicy dishes all the time, one needs ever more spices to taste anything at all. The same is true for the other senses. By indulging oneself, one needs a higher and higher dose to be stimulated. A cycle of addiction is easily established. The sage, on the other hand, aims at keeping a taste for the tasteless. If one is able to appreciate the slightest stimulation, one keeps the ability to be sensitive to nuances—and thus remains or returns to the state of an infant (see chapter 10). Similarly, exciting activities like galloping or hunting and the striving for precious things wearies one's mind. One loses the capacity for simple satisfaction.

The sage ruler will have to take this aspect of human character into account and not allow for too much sensual, or other, excess. He has to keep the population satisfied—bellies have to be filled, but luxury goods are not displayed (see chapter 3). Everything that stirs up the people's feelings, ambitions, or minds should be avoided. The Daoist state is certainly not a consumer society. For the sake of general satisfaction the spectacular and the exciting are prevented from disturbing society's peace.

Twelve

十二

The five colors
      make one's eyes blind.
Galloping horses and hunting in the fields
      make one's heart mad.
Goods that are difficult to obtain
      obstruct one's ways.
The five tastes
      make one's palate obtuse.
The five tones
      make one's ears deaf.

Therefore the sage orders like this:
      He cares for the belly, not for the eye.
      Thus he gets rid of that and chooses this.

instinct

Commentary on Chapter Thirteen

This chapter intertwines two Daoist topics. The first is the emotional equanimity of the sage ruler who is touched by neither the favors bestowed on him nor the disgraces that he might be exposed to. The second is the sage ruler's care for his own body. The text says that the ruler will not welcome any favors because this might infringe upon his impartiality. Moreover, to receive a favor or gift from someone establishes a sort of dependency. To receive something from someone creates an obligation and establishes a relation of indebtedness. Also, a favor may be withdrawn and this establishes another sort of dependency. The sage ruler is supposed to treat everyone equally and not to be biased, so he cannot allow himself to receive favors and thus, implicitly, to grant special treatment to some and not to others. It can be inferred that the same logic also applies to disgrace. The sage does not take anything personally (since he is void of a personality—of personal feelings, inclinations, or desires). He can be neither flattered by gifts nor taken aback by personal offences.

What the ruler has to take care of, however, is his body. In a paradoxical way the ruler's care for his body—and not for political power—makes him the ideal ruler in the state. This logic is reminiscent of the Daoist "heretic" Yang Zhu who, so the legend goes, would not give a single hair in exchange for becoming the ruler of the world. To keep one's body intact was seen as an indicator of being in harmony with the Dao. The body is a well-functioning natural scenario, and if we are able to care for it, we have obviously mastered the technique of being in harmony with nature or the Dao. This view was crucial for later developments in practical or religious Daoism, which put so much emphasis on bodily cultivation. Other parts of the *Daodejing*, for instance, chapters 10 and 54, address this topic as well. To take care of one's body does not mean to be selfish—it means quite the opposite, namely, to minimize one's desires (for such things as power and wealth) and withdraw from social competition. Not unlike

Socrates' teaching in Plato's *Republic*, it is this personal disinterest in power that makes one so suitable for being a ruler. Only by having no personal interest in ruling will one not be prone to use power for selfish pursuits or personal gain. The one who is least interested in ruling will make the most impartial and unbiased leader.

It is interesting to take a closer look at the literary structure of this chapter. The first two sentences sound like common folk sayings. The rest of the chapter is structured in parallelisms and provides short "philosophical" explanations of the two sayings. This structure demonstrates the likelihood of an initial oral transmission of the text. It looks as if the Daoists collected such sayings and then attached poetical-philosophical interpretations to them.

Thirteen

十三

A favor as well as a disgrace will make you alarmed.
Esteem your body with great worries.

What does it mean:
     "A favor as well as a disgrace will make you alarmed"?
To be given a favor is to be an underling.
To receive it will make you alarmed.
To lose it will make you alarmed.
This means:
     A favor as well as a disgrace will make you alarmed.

What does it mean:
     "Esteem your body with great worries"?
The reason why I have great worries
     is that I have a body.
If I did not have a body,
     what worry would I have?

Thus,
     if you esteem taking care of your body more than you
       do taking care of the world,
     then you can be entrusted with the world;
     if you love your body as if it were the world,
     then the world can be handed over to you.

Commentary on Chapter Fourteen

The first three lines describe the Dao in the style of a riddle. The Dao is that which is so minute that it is invisible, so quiet that it is silent, so ungraspable that it is perfectly smooth. These three negative characteristics of the Dao correspond to or are associated with its central quality of being empty. That which is empty is without shape, without sound, and without tactile features. It should be noted that the Dao is not—unlike God—"beyond" any form, shape, or description, but rather "below" it. It does not escape definition because of any "supernatural" nature, but rather by its natural emptiness. Like the hub within a wheel, it simply has no positive features.

The second stanza has to be understood in the context of ancient Chinese numerology. Both the number one and the number three symbolize unity or oneness. The blending of threeness results in oneness. The Dao is, like a hub, the "empty" inner unity of the cosmic functioning. But by uniting the cosmos it also provides for the "full" oneness of the cosmic "wheel," that is, the cosmic process as a unified scenario. The Dao is thus both single (like a hub) and total (like the wheel). Like the number one it is both the smallest in number and the number of the whole. Its singleness and totality are the two complementary forms of its oneness. It includes "darkness" and "brightness," or the Yin and Yang aspects of the cosmic cycle, and combines them into one process. Both with respect to its single emptiness and total fullness, the Dao is shapeless; it is no specific thing. It is as empty and vast as a barren desert.

The last stanza is once more reminiscent of a riddle in style. If one follows it, one doesn't see its back, if one approaches it, one doesn't see its front. The Dao is continuously on the move; it is a way that continuously unfolds. But due to its emptiness and ultimate fullness it has no specific front or back, it has no shape or individual features. As the permanent course of change, it escapes any specific determination and is as much in the past as it is in the present. All in all, the text of this chapter describes in its typically elusive and alluding fashion the Dao as the total process of change or "thread" that is, paradoxically, not identifiable with any of the particularities or segments that constitute it. It is both the inner and outer, both the minimal and maximal unit.

Fourteen

十四

That which one looks at but does not see,
    it is named "minute."
That which one listens to but does not hear,
    it is named "silent."
That which one holds but does not get,
    it is named "smooth."

These three—
    cannot not be ultimately calculated.
    Thus they are mixed and become one.
The one—
    above it, it isn't bright,
    below it, it isn't dark.
This is called:
    shape without shape,
    figure without thing.
This is called:
    barrenness, desert.

Follow it—
    and you don't see its back.
Approach it—
    and you don't see its head.
Grasp the Dao of today—
    in order to manage what is present today,
    in order to know the beginning in antiquity.
This is called: "thread of the Dao."

Commentary on Chapter Fifteen

This chapter can be read as a poetic and again cryptic description of the Daoist sage or sage ruler: "those who were good at practicing the Dao." These rulers date back to antiquity, and the Daoists share this motif of worshipping the past with the Confucians. But, unlike the legendary Confucian sage rulers, the Daoist ones lack specific characteristics. They only have the typical Daoist noncharacteristics: they are secret and subtle, dark and thorough, deep and unfathomable. And if one is to describe them, only vague and dark terms can be applied —as the second stanza does. Here there are a number of images, many of them having to do with water. These images evoke carefulness, rawness, and smoothness. It seems that the sages were sparing in their actions and treated things with great caution. The last stanza talks about the muddy becoming clear and then alive. Once more, the image of water is evoked and associated with the generation of life. The last two lines are difficult to interpret, particularly in the versions of the Mawangdui manuscripts which have "incomplete" instead of "renewed" in the standard text. In this instance, the standard version makes more sense and would say that sages—like doors or jugs—are not easily worn out.

Fifteen

十五

Of those in antiquity who were good at practicing the Dao:
    secret and subtle,
    dark and thorough,
    so deep as to be unfathomable.
Well,
    just because they are unfathomable,
    one has to be forced to give a description of them:

How cautious!
    Like crossing a river in the winter.
How careful!
    Like being afraid of the neighbors on the four sides.
How earnest!
    Like being a guest.
How loosening!
    Like melting ice.
How raw!
    Like uncarved wood.
How impenetrable!
    Like muddy water.
How vast!
    Like the valley.

If that which is turbid is kept still, it will gradually clear up.
If it is moved, it will gradually come alive.
Those who hold on to this Dao
    do not desire the filled.
Therefore
    they can be worn out and incomplete.

Commentary on Chapter Sixteen

This chapter combines three main Daoist images or topics: emptiness, stillness, and permanence. The Daoist sage or sage ruler manifests emptiness and stillness, or the Dao, and thereby establishes permanence. The same permanence that prevails in nature can, through the nonaction of the sage ruler, also "bless" humankind.

I think that the "I" at the beginning of the second stanza is the "I" of the sage ruler who is the "reader" addressed by the text. It is through this "I" that the prospective sage ruler identifies himself with the Daoist "message" and strategy. It is stated that the things in the world turn to stillness—or to the "root," to express it with another favorite image in the *Daodejing*. The cycle of life returns to death in order to begin anew. Stillness allows for constant return and thus for an ongoing permanence. This is natural, and the Daoists would like to bring this natural permanence into the social realm. The sage ruler thus has to study natural cycles of permanence: the yearly "return" of the plants, for instance, which sustains life in an agricultural society—or the returning course of the "heavenly" (celestial) bodies that establishes the yearly sequence of time. To know and master permanence qualifies one for being a sage ruler. If one is unable to know and master permanence one will give rise to disasters and catastrophes by not being in tune with nature and "heaven"—one will be a ruler who attracts bad luck and misfortunes.

The final lines of the chapter describe the mastery of permanence as the key to "good government" in harmony with the Dao. One who is in harmony with the Dao may not be endangered by the transitoriness of time. This may mean, analogous to the mastery of permanence, that a sage ruler's state will endure, or it may mean that the sage ruler will not fear death. A reading more in line with later Daoist longevity practices would be that the sage ruler is such a great master of permanence that he will actually become immortal.

Sixteen

十六

To reach emptiness—
    this is the utmost.
To keep stillness—
    this is control.

The ten thousand things occur along with each other:
    So I watch where they turn.
The things in the world are manifold,
    they all return again to their root:
    "stillness."
"Stillness"—this is what the return to the mandate is called.
The return to the mandate—this is permanence.
To know permanence—this is clarity.
To not know permanence—this is error.
With errors the unfortunate occurs.
To know permanence is to be incorporating.
To be incorporating is rulership.
Rulership is kingship.
Kingship is heavenly.
Heavenly is the Dao.
The Dao is
    not to be endangered by the decay of the body.

Commentary on Chapter Seventeen

The first stanza of this chapter is quite straightforward about the Daoist art of rulership. The ideal ruler is one who is not, or only hardly, noticed by his subjects. He remains unseen and nonactive, and thus he will not be the slightest burden on the people. This effect is echoed in the last stanza that states that people will perfectly perform their duties without even knowing of the government and its orders. They fulfill their respective duties simply "self-so," or naturally or spontaneously (*ziran*).

The Daoist art of rulership is thus superior to a Confucian type of government, namely, government by the worthy who are respected and loved by their subjects. Affection for one's ruler is not as stable as the absence of any emotional bond between the ruler and the ruled. Emotional investment may make the ruler partial and subject to personal feelings and inclinations. The Daoist sage ruler remains entirely "cool"—he does not reign out of affection but simply in accordance with the principle of nonaction so that the people will do what is right "automatically." This kind of rulership is more permanent than a rule based on fragile emotions.

The third best ruler is a Legalist who rules through coercion. This kind of rule is a negative mirror image of the Confucian type of government. Here, there is also an emotional relation between the ruler and the ruled, albeit not one of affection. The Legalist ruler rules through punishment and reward. Everyone tries to avoid punishment while attempting to be rewarded. This results in a culture of mistrust and competitiveness, and most of all, in pervasive anxiety. Like in the Confucian model, the Legalist type of government is highly emotional. Here, however, people will be obedient not out of affection but—which is even more unstable—out of fear of punishment.

The Confucian and Legalist rule, however, may still work for a period of time even though they are, after Daoist rule, the "next best" forms of government. Only the last type of rule mentioned in this chapter is wholly dysfunctional. A ruler who is not taken seriously by his subjects lacks all authority and is thus, in the strict sense of the term, not a ruler at all. His government is bound to fail.

What the second stanza seems to be saying is that, unlike the Confucian ruler, the Daoist sage does not establish his rule on trustworthiness. Like affection, trustworthiness is an ambiguous virtue that creates problems in the long run. When there is trustworthiness, there is also the possibility of mistrust. It is better for the ruler to be silent or spare with words than for him to rely on trustworthy pronouncements.

Seventeen

十七

Of the best of all rulers
> people will only know that he exists.
The next best
> they will praise with affection.
The next best
> they will fear.
The worst
> will be ridiculed.

If trustworthiness does not suffice,
> there will be untrustworthiness.
How cautious he is—
> how he esteems words!

The works are completed,
The tasks are followed through.
> And the people declare:
> "It happens to us 'self-so.'"

Commentary on Chapter Eighteen

This chapter continues the discourse on Daoist rulership that began in the previous chapter and is carried over into the following one. Even more bluntly than chapter 17 here the Confucian virtues are decried as ineffective and dangerous virtues of latecomers. They only apply when a state of decay has already been established. The Confucian "cures" for a corrupt state are comparable to a doctor's prescription that takes care only of the symptoms of an illness while doing nothing to prevent its occurrence.

As was the case in the previous chapter, here the ambiguous character of the Confucian virtues is criticized. With the establishment of such "positive" values as humanity (*ren*), righteousness (*yi*), knowledge (*zhi*), and filial piety (*xiao*), the Confucians also implicitly create their opposites. Once there is righteousness, there is not only the possibility of being unrighteous, but also a continuous quarrel about what is righteous. In comparison with the Daoist negative ethics of nonaction, Confucian positive ethics create the conditions not only for immorality, but also for an ongoing dispute about what is ethical. Those who feel that they are righteous may well feel that others are not and need to be punished. The trouble is, however, that the "unrighteous" will most likely also think themselves in the right. Moral, political, and even military conflicts are not far apart from each other. In fact, they often arise together and fuel one another.

Eighteen

十八

Thus,
When the great Dao is dispensed with,
    then there is humanity and righteousness.
When knowledge and smartness come out,
    then there is great falsity.
When the six family relations are not harmonious,
    then there is filial piety and compassion.
When state and families are in confusion,
    then there are upright ministers.

Commentary on Chapter Nineteen

This translation of chapter 19 represents the version of the text that is found in the Mawangdui manuscripts. Other versions vary quite significantly. (See the appendix for a detailed analysis of these variants and a hypothesis on the evolution of the text.)

If this reading is accepted, then the chapter continues and even amplifies the anti-Confucian polemics of the two preceding chapters. The first three sentences are parallel in style and content. They denounce the Confucian virtues and ask for their elimination. The Confucian virtues are seen as obstacles to the creation of a good society. Rather than bettering the world, they contribute to the evils they are supposed to remedy.

The second verse seems to refer to the first three sentences as three more or less commonly known sayings that, for the sake of poetic and semantic parallelism, should be followed by three more sayings that will complement the mere criticism of Confucian values with a Daoist message. "Plainness" (*su*) and "simplicity" (*pu*) are Daoist "countervirtues" that are supposed to replace the discarded Confucian ethics. Instead of cultivating human morality, the Daoist sage cultivates a more natural way of being that is void of Confucian adornments. The Daoist "negative" virtues are obviously nonhumanist. They aim at curbing particularly human qualities and allow for a reversion to a more original form of existence that has not yet developed a need for moral codes and regulations, a premoral social state in which people act harmoniously self-so (*ziran*) without a need for ethical instructions and prescriptions.

Nineteen

十九

Abandon sageliness and discard knowledge,
    and the people will benefit a hundredfold.
Abandon humanity and discard righteousness,
    and the people will return to filial piety and care.
Abandon skill and discard profit,
    and there will be no thieves or robbers.

These three sayings:
    They are not yet sufficient for forming a pattern,
    thus they shall be connected with something.

Manifest plainness, embrace simplicity,
reduce selfishness, have less desires,
abandon learning, have no worries.

Commentary on Chapter Twenty

This chapter is one of the literary gems of the Daodejing. With intense imagery it contrasts the qualities of the common people with the Daoist sage ruler. The common people are active and subject to emotions and moods. In their duties and festivities they are also subject to differences and particularities. They live in a world of complementary opposites. They approve and disapprove, like and dislike. They have fears and hopes, joys and worries. Thus they are different from the sage ruler who is without any particular feeling or personality. He is without shape and form, like an endless ocean or a barren desert. Endlessness and barrenness, solitariness and indistinctness, indifference and untouchability, and permanence and hiddenness are the typical "negative" features of the Daoist sage. These are combined in this chapter with the images of the newly born infant (or the embryo) and the idiot. The infant has not yet developed a personality; it does not yet have an ego or individual qualities. It is in a yet undifferentiated state void of particular mental contents—it is perfectly "idiotic." The sage ruler is able to return to this state in which he only "esteems the nurturing mother" (the Dao or nature) and has no other desire than to be in accordance and harmony with her.

Twenty

二十

To agree politely and to reject angrily—
      how far are they apart from each other?
To find something beautiful and to find something ugly—
      in which way are these apart from each other?
If you are feared by others,
      you will accordingly not be able to not fear them.

What desert! It never comes to an end!
The ordinary people are in a good mood—
      as if celebrating a great sacrifice
      or climbing the terraces in the spring.
I am serenely among them and do not show any sign,
      like an infant that does not yet smile.
What tiredness! As if there is no place to return to.
The ordinary people all have in abundance—
I alone have abandoned.
I have the heart of an idiot.

What simplicity!
The ordinary people are shining—
I alone seem to be hidden.
The ordinary people are distinct—
I alone am undifferentiated.
What barrenness! It is like the ocean.
What desert! As if it will never stop.
The ordinary people all have their purposes—
I alone am so stupid, to the degree of a yokel.
My desires alone are different from those of the other people—
      and I esteem the nurturing mother.

51

Commentary on Chapter Twenty-one

The images of barrenness and the desert that appear here were introduced in the preceding chapter. They are part of the group of images that depict the Dao's shapelessness and endlessness. The Dao is that which has not yet taken on shape, it is the "uncarved wood" (*pu*, see chapters 15, 28, 32, and 37, also translated as "simplicity," see chapters 19, and 57). "In the midst" of the formless are the forms—the "figures," "things," and "seminal energies,"—that are implicit in the yet-uncarved wood like all the potential forms. In taking on shapes and forms, the Dao unfolds its "efficacy" or "power" (*de*) that, in turn, only "follows" the Dao.

That which has taken on forms and shapes is that which is named. It is named precisely because it has specific features and thus can be given specific designations. The realm of the ten thousand things is the realm of the named, of that which has taken on form from the formless. The Dao is, in this respect, the "father of all." Other chapters (1, 20, 25, 52, and 59) speak of the Dao as the mother, which is the more frequently used term, keeping in line with the *Daodejing*'s preference of feminine imagery.

It is tempting, but not binding, to read this and other chapters that present the Dao as "father" or "mother" of all in a metaphysical or even theological fashion and to understand the Dao as an absolute origin of the world. However, the Dao and the ten thousand things—at least in my interpretation—can also be conceived of as co-emerging. The Dao is the unspecific totality of all the specific, the grand scenario that allows everything within it to emerge in its respective specificity. Rather than being a Godlike creator, the Dao is, like the root (see chapters 6 and 16), the "dark" source out of which everything that can be seen emerges, but is not essentially different from it.

Twenty-one

二十一

Grand efficacy's manner
>   follows only the Dao.
The thing Dao—only desert, only barren.

What barrenness, what desert!
>   In their midst are the figures.
What barrenness, what desert!
>   In their midst are the things.
What nebulosity, what obscurity!
>   And what seminal energies in their midst!
>   The seminal energies are very genuine.
Therein is trustworthiness.

From today to antiquity
>   their names have not been taken away
in order to follow the father of all.
How do I know what the father of all is?
Thus.

Commentary on Chapter Twenty-two

The first stanza of this chapter is a collection of Daoist paradoxes. These can be understood as temporal and sequential—for instance one may think of a bow that is drawn and then released, or of a plant that is "worn out" in the winter and then grows anew in the spring. The course of the Dao is one in which things change into their opposites just as the positions of spokes change when a wheel is in motion. Within this course of change the sage holds on to or manifests the "one," that is, the inner and outer unity of the whole. He is the hub that unites the course of the revolving spokes. To hold on to the one is to fit seemingly separate and diverse elements into a unified scenario—like the hub that unites the separate spokes into one wheel. This is the working of the Dao; it is that which unites all the separate elements in nature into a single, permanent, and circular process of time. The last stanza seems to respond to the first one. It complements the first while adding one important Daoist notion, namely "return." The course of time, like that of a wheel, is one of circular return within which things change into their opposites and then back into what they were before. Wholeness is constituted by return—like the drawing of a circle.

The middle portion of the chapter "translates" the paradoxical pattern of the temporal course of nature into a strategy for ruling and for acquiring and holding on to political power. The Daoist sage ruler rules by retreat. He manages to keep his position and to stabilize the state through noninterference. The ideal ruler—of whom chapter 17 said that people only know of his existence—remains invisible and thus immune from confrontation and loss of prestige. The last line in this stanza once more emphasizes that these negative "virtues" of the sage ruler result in permanence: they allow him and the state to "last long." One additional aspect of this art of long-lasting rulership is the absence of a struggle for power. The ruler's retreat makes him invulnerable and his radical "modesty" (he does not portray himself as a good ruler and does not strive for power) results in a perfect lack of political contention.

Twenty-two

二十二

Flexed then whole,
bent then upright,
hollow then full,
worn out then new,
little then gaining,
much then confused.

Therefore,
>the sage holds on to oneness
>to be the shepherd of the world.

He does not make himself shown,
>and thus he is apparent.
He does not make himself seen,
>and thus he shines.
He does not acclaim himself,
>and thus he has success.
He is not conceited,
>and thus he can last long.

Well,
>it is because only he does not struggle
>that nobody can struggle with him.

What in antiquity was said with respect to the flexed and the
>whole—
>>weren't these words that came close?
To the truly whole—this is where it returns.

Commentary on Chapter Twenty-three

This chapter consists of three quite separate parts. The first has only four characters and states rather sparingly that being spare with words is "natural" or "self-so" (*ziran*)—at least for the sage ruler or the Dao. It is not only that "heaven" does not speak (to use the words of Confucius in *Analects* 17.19); even the sage who is in accord with the Dao keeps silent. This line connects with the theme of the sage ruler's retreat in the preceding chapter.

The second stanza speaks of unfortunate events in nature—whirlwinds and downpours—that could destroy crops and ruin the harvest. Even nature, it seems, is not always productive and timely. Something as fruitful and nourishing as rain can, at times, create a devastating flood. Clouds and rain (a Chinese metaphor for sexuality) are not only sources of fertility but, when nature operates "out of order," can take on the form of natural disasters or catastrophes. These events, however, never "last long." They are not elements of permanence, but interruptions to (and eruptions of) the steady course of time. The course of time (and thus of the Dao) is under the constant threat of being obstructed, but these obstructions cannot be constant. They occur, but cannot continue for long. Translated into political doctrine this means that an "eruptive," active leader who attempts to forcefully interfere with the "natural" order will ultimately be unable to succeed. If even the forces of nature cannot interrupt the course of the Dao for long, the chapter asks rhetorically, how could humans? While there is always the possibility of the natural course of things being harmed, such violence never lasts.

The third stanza plays with the homophonous but differently written words for "efficacy" (*de*) and "to receive" or "to gain" (*de*). Since the play on words is difficult to represent in English, I have chosen to translate this passage rather freely. What the stanza seems to be saying—in loose connection with the preceding stanza—is that the course of the Dao and the unfolding of its efficacy (*de*) is based on a rhythmical pattern of gain and loss. When it rains the sky "looses" (*shi*) its water and the earth "gains" it which allows for things to grow. When the Dao is established, its course unfolds as gain and loss or, as I have translated the terms here, as giving and taking. What looses (*shi*) gives, and what gains (*de*) takes. If giving and taking function in accord with the Dao, this will result in fertility and production.

Twenty-three

二十三

Silent speech—self-so.

A whirlwind does not last a morning.
    A downpour does not last a day.
Who is acting in these cases?
        Heaven and earth—
        but even these can't make them last.
How then, should humans be able to?

Thus follow the task and
        the Dao is in accord with the Dao,
        what takes accords with taking,
        what gives accords with giving.
When the taking is in accord, the Dao takes too.
When the giving is in accord, the Dao gives too.

Commentary on Chapter Twenty-four

This second stanza of this chapter almost repeats a series of sayings from chapter 22. The ruler who exposes himself to the public and who is boastful and glitzy—or, as one would say in our times, who indulges in a cult of personality—is bound to fail. Such excessive manners will result in arrogance and vulnerability and the ruler will ultimately be despised. One may well read this chapter as a general call to modesty—a call to modesty for the sake of one's sanity. The desire for glamour and show should be restrained for one's own good.

•

Twenty-four

二 十 四

The boastful do not stand fast.

One who makes oneself shown
     is not apparent.
One who makes oneself seen
     does not shine.
One who acclaims oneself
     has no success.
One who is conceited
     cannot last long.

With respect to the Dao this is to say:
     "overindulgence in food and excessive ado."
This is generally despised.
Thus the one who desires it will not dwell there.

Commentary on Chapter Twenty-five

The first stanza of chapter 25 is strongly reminiscent of chapter 21. The imagery of shapelessness and vastness reoccurs here along with the imagery of the "parenthood" of the Dao, although it appears here not as the "father of all" but as "the mother to heaven and earth." Philosophically this may be interpreted in the same way I read chapter 21. That is to say, the Dao does not appear as a detached origin but as an inseparable source that is integrated in its "offspring." The Dao is unchanging—but in the paradoxical language of Daoism this means: it is the unchanging change, the permanence of the impermanent, the cyclical course of time that goes on endlessly but consists of temporal and passing segments of time.

The second stanza discusses once more the namelessness of the Dao (see, for instance, chapter 1). Since it has no specific characteristics, the Dao cannot be named. If we still call it "greatness," we will have to take into account that this entails a paradoxical aspect. As a circular movement, the Dao returns to its beginning. The Dao is the great circle of time and procreation that progresses backwards. This circle includes the social world—the world of the "king"—as well as the natural world. Human life is integrated in the yearly cycle that is constituted by the "earth" (the growth and withering of the plants) and "heaven" (the course of the seasons and of the heavenly bodies). Taken together, humans, earth, and heaven constitute the scenario of the Dao. This scenario is not modeled on some higher law or metaphysical principle; rather, it follows its own course—it is how it is simply "self-so" (*ziran*). With its final line the chapter thus highlights the central importance of the notion of "self-so" in Daoism. Again it becomes obvious that the philosophy of the *Daodejing* is one of immanence. There is nothing "behind" the Dao. The Dao is simply the course of nature that goes on by itself.

Twenty-five

二十五

There is a thing—
> it came to be in the undifferentiated,
> it came alive before heaven and earth.
What stillness! What emptiness!
Alone it stands fast and does not change.
It can be mother to heaven and earth.

I do not know its name.
It is called Dao.
If I was forced to name it,
> I would say "Greatness."
"Greatness" means "to proceed."
"To proceed" means "distance."
"Distance" means "return."

The Dao is great.
Heaven is great.
The earth is great.
The king is also great.
In the land there are four greats—
> and the king positions himself where they are one.
Humans follow the earth as a rule.
The earth follows heaven as a rule.
Heaven follows the Dao as a rule.
The Dao follows its self-so as a rule.

Commentary on Chapter Twenty-six

The first two sayings of this chapter discuss two related Daoist maxims. The first is that one should not neglect indicators and the second is the well-known teaching of nonaction. With regard to the first saying, Daoists emphasize that developments, particularly those leading to negative effects such as disasters or illnesses, can usually be detected early on. One can see that the crops are not growing well before the harvest is ruined, and one can be watchful for unhealthy symptoms in the body well before a deadly disease has developed. Likewise, a political crisis begins with signs of discontent and social unrest. This chapter seems to emphasize that prevention is more effective than dealing with a full-grown calamity. It is better, then, to take things seriously. One has to watch the course things take so that aberrations can be prevented. This teaching resonates with the Daoist insistence on taking care of one's own body (compare also chapter 13). The body of a person is the organism that is closest at hand. If a person is unable to bring order to the body and maintain its efficacy, then he or she will hardly be able to take care of a larger body such as the political body (the state) or the cosmic body (the course of nature). If one is watchful of one's body and good at recognizing the early indicators of malfunctions, one will have the necessary sensitivity to notice when things in society and nature begin to go wrong. Along this sense, a Daoist sage will be, of course, spare with his actions and not be agitated or agitating. Caring for an organism by preventive methods requires less effort than caring for it by fighting against problems that have already developed. The least amount of action and agitation is needed at the earliest stages. If one takes small things seriously, one needs to take little action to cope with them.

The second stanza is difficult to interpret. It may say in an allegorical fashion that the sage ruler does not leave his place. Not going far is certainly a Daoist virtue (see chapters 47 and 80), so, even when traveling, the ruler will minimize his activity and remain in solitude.

Twenty-six

二十六

Taking gravely is the root of taking lightly.
Stillness is the master of agitation.

Therefore the gentleman,
    when he travels all day,
    will not go far from his luggage carts.
Even when there is a hostel available
    he remains where it is quiet
    so that he maintains his loftiness.

What king of ten thousand chariots is this
    who takes his body more lightly than the world?
If one takes things lightly, then the root is lost.
If one is agitated, rulership is lost.

Commentary on Chapter Twenty-seven

Being able to leave no trace is a motif that Daoism and Chan (or Zen) Buddhism share. There is a Zen Buddhist legend of a certain kind of antelope that sleeps hanging from a tree in order not to leave any trace on the ground. Leaving no trace is an indicator of the total absence of friction—one who does not leave a trace is in perfect accord with the environment and does not impose anything on it. This motif corresponds with chapter 17, which states that the best ruler goes practically unnoticed by his people. Leaving no trace in society, he does not interfere in their affairs and does not attempt to impose anything on them. He just lets things unfold naturally. This is his way of "going" or acting. To leave no trace is a poetic formula for the famous Daoist maxim of doing nothing while leaving nothing undone (*wu wei er wu bu wei*). By not interfering and leaving no trace, the sage ruler remains flawless and rules effortlessly: he does not need any instrument for "calculating" what to do.

The tracelessness, flawlessness, and effortlessness of the sage ruler integrates him perfectly into society and nature. There is no place where this perfect union could be unlocked or untied. The sage ruler fits seamlessly into the state and into the cosmos. Everything is included in this scenario; no people or goods remain outside.

The third stanza is somewhat Confucian in tone. There is a saying in the *Analects* (7.22) that reads: "The Master said: 'In strolling in the company of just two other persons, I am bound to find a teacher. Identifying their strengths, I follow them, and identifying their weaknesses, I reform myself accordingly.'"[4] It seems that both passages convey the same message and may, in fact, have a common source in some popular saying. There is always something one can learn from a good person as well as, if only negatively, from a bad one.

---

4. Roger T. Ames and Henry Rosemont Jr., *The Analects of Confucius: A Philosophical Translation* (New York: Ballantine, 1998), 116.

Twenty-seven

二十七

One who is good at going does not leave traces.
One who is good at speaking remains without flaws.
One who is good at calculating does not use counting chips.
That which is well locked has no bolts and cannot be opened.
That which is well tied has no cords and cannot be undone.

Therefore the sage
    is constantly good at assisting the people
    and does not abandon them.
As to the things, he does not abandon that which is valuable.
This is called "multiple clarity."

Thus,
    A person who is good
        is a teacher for the good person.
    A person who is not good
        is a valuable object for the good person.
One who does not esteem the teachers and does not cherish
  the valuable objects
    will be, even though he might be knowledgeable,
        greatly misled.
This is called "the essential of the subtle."

Commentary on Chapter Twenty-eight

The first three stanzas of this chapter are a rhythmical, parallel poem that, at least partially, rhymes. Semantically, it combines many core Daoist images, among them the valley (see chapters 6 and 39), the infant (see chapter 55), and the uncarved wood (see chapters 15, 32, and 37). Along with these images, there occur equally important Daoist conceptual pairs: male/female, white/black (brightness/darkness), and immaculate/muddled, as well as the prominent notion of "efficacy" or *de*. The chapter thus presents a dense collage of Daoist motifs that reappear in the same or similar forms throughout the text. To explain them (and thus the chapter) one has to understand the general sense of such imagery. The infant, the valley, and the uncarved wood are all images of unspent and untiring potentiality or fertility. They are symbols of the productive nature of the Dao. The conceptual pairs or "dualisms"—in correspondence with the rhythmical nature of the verses—represent the rhythm of Yin and Yang that constitutes the Dao. The female and the male, or darkness and brightness, are the two aspects of the process of procreation and the unfolding time. Speaking in the numerical language of chapter 42, the valley, the infant, and the uncarved wood represent the "oneness" associated with the Dao, while the dualistic pairs represent its "twoness." In combination, the oneness and the twoness give rise to the Dao's efficacy or "power" (*de*).

By focusing on the respective final sentences of the first three stanzas, this chapter can be read as a guide for the prospective ruler. He is supposed to reach the states of oneness—or to "return to the state of infancy." The infant is without self-consciousness and lives in "instinctive" nonaction. It is perfectly "self-so." This state is reached by a "return," and the power or efficacy of this state is said to be "constant"—two further core notions in the *Daodejing*.

The last stanza is poetically and semantically different from the preceding ones. It is connected to them, however, through the image of the uncarved wood. This analogy may, perhaps, have caused the editors of the text to group these two textual segments together. This last part of the text is political in tone. It portrays the Daoist state as a whole that is united and produced by the ruler, the uncarved wood. The ruler is thus the "one body" that integrates the whole of society.

Twenty-eight

二十八

Know the masculine and maintain the feminine—
    be the world's river.
Be the world's river
    and constant efficacy won't leave you.
If the constant efficacy does not leave you,
    you return to the state of infancy.

Know the world's immaculateness and maintain the
  muddled—
    be the world's valley.
Be the world's valley,
    and constant efficacy will suffice.
When constant efficacy suffices,
    you will return again to the state of uncarved wood.

Know the world's white and maintain the black—
    be the world's pattern.
Be the world's pattern,
    and constant efficacy will be unharmed.
When constant efficacy is unharmed,
    you will return again to the boundless.

When the uncarved wood is parted,
    then tools come into being.
When the sage makes use of them,
    he becomes the leader of all officials.
Well, great woodcarving does not carve anything off.

Commentary on Chapter Twenty-nine

The two stanzas of this chapter are quite different from one another. The first is one of the most explicit formulations of the maxim of *wu wei*, or nonaction, in the *Daodejing*. It is quite obviously addressed to a prospective ruler who "wants to take hold of the world." One acquires and maintains political power through passivity. Active approaches cause social friction and antagonisms and are ultimately bound to fail.

The second stanza is more difficult to interpret. There are two statements, one about the "things" and the other about the sage, each of which consists of three parallel lines that comment on their respective topics. This stylistic parallelism might have been the reason why the two statements are grouped together. The saying about the "things" seems to describe complementary patterns in the world of the manifold. The Dao is a rhythmic course within which things rise and fall—like the spokes of a wheel, to cite the crucial image that occurs in chapter 11. The world of concrete things and events is thus a process of motion in which things follow each other—again like the spokes of a wheel. The "burning" and "breaking" of which the second line speaks may indicate that in the course of change, the individual elements are subject to decay—and are replaced by new things. The course as such is permanent, but the individual segments are not.

The final statement is reminiscent of other passages (for instance, in chapter 39) that discuss the "modesty" of the sage ruler. The ruler does not stand out. He retreats and is perfectly frugal. There is nothing extravagant or peculiar about him—he is without any quality.

Twenty-nine

二十九

If one wants to take hold of the world,
> and act on it—
I see that he will not succeed.
Well,
> the world is a sacred vessel,
> and not something that can be acted on.
Those who act on things will be defeated by them.
Those who take things in their hands will lose them.

The things:
> some go, some follow,
> some burn, some break,
> some rise, some fall.
Therefore the sage
> discards the excessive,
> discards the great,
> discards the extraordinary.

Commentary on Chapter Thirty

The first and second stanzas resonate with the pacifist tone of the following chapter. War is destructive, it kills people and ruins the fields, and thus the sage ruler tries to avoid it altogether. In fact, political stability depends on the absence of war. Therefore it is one of the main tasks of the ruler to prevent war from happening. The use of force is always a bad way of acting and when he is unable to avoid war, the sage ruler uses defensive and evasive tactics to keep losses at a minimum.

Like the last section of the previous chapter, the third stanza depicts the modesty of the sage ruler. The ideal ruler remains hidden and does not show off. He does not even keep any possessions. He possesses nothing in particular and thereby there is nothing that he does not possess. The sage ruler's aversion to war goes along with his absence of self-aggrandizement and yearning for goods. He aspires for neither fame nor wealth. These aspirations are among the main reasons for war, and when rulers do not have them, war becomes less likely.

The last stanza rhymes. Its meaning, however, is not entirely clear. What it might say is that an early and untimely end, or premature aging, is not in line with the Dao. The Dao is the natural process things take. If energies are squandered, for instance through the use of force or warfare, things cannot live out their proper lifespan. They will not last as long as they would have if they acted sparingly. This same stanza reoccurs at the end of chapter 55.

Thirty

三十

When the ruler of people is assisted by the Dao
  then the force of weapons is not used in the world.

Such affairs like to turn around:
  Where armies were placed
  grow thorns and brushes.

The one who is good has success—
  that is all.
He does not use force to get it.
He has success and is not proud.
He has success and is not arrogant.
He has success and does not brag.
He has success and does not get anything with which he
 would abide.
This is called: "He has success without using force."

If a thing grows up and then gets old,
  this is called "not the Dao."
"Not the Dao" ends early.

Commentary on Chapter Thirty-one

There has been much speculation about the authenticity of this chapter, partly due to the fact that it is one of only two that lack a commentary in Wang Bi's (226–249 CE) standard edition of the text. Some scholars believed that Wang had in fact written a commentary that was later erroneously amalgamated into the chapter. This theory is used to explain why the chapter reads somewhat strangely. The Mawangdui manuscripts (that predate Wang Bi's edition by nearly half a millennium), however, include the chapter in full so that it is now clear that this hypothesis is false.

The chapter is quite Confucian in tone. It is the only chapter in the *Daodejing* that mentions the "noble man" (*junzi*), an ideal of personhood that appears very frequently in Confucian texts. It also discusses ritual procedures, which is much more typical of Confucian philosophical literature.

The passage on rites points out that the left side (in a ritual ceremony) is associated with the auspicious whereas the right side is associated with the inauspicious. Weapons are said to be of "ill omen" and so war, consequently, corresponds to the "right." In line with the preceding chapter, war is regarded as a great calamity and social catastrophe. Therefore the Daoist ruler treats it as an event of sorrow and grief—and not as an occasion for triumph or delight. War is always a result of failed politics and even a successful war is costly in both lives and material.

Thirty-one

三十一

Weapons are the tools of ill omen.
Generally they are loathed.
Thus one who has intentions will not reside with them.
When the noble man is at his residence
     he esteems the left.
When the noble man makes use of the military
     he esteems the right.
Thus,
weapons are not the tools of the noble man.
Weapons are the tools of ill omen.
When he cannot do otherwise, he uses them—
     to him staying calm is the best.
Do not regard them with delight.
To regard them with delight—
     this is to enjoy the killing of people.
Well, by enjoying the killing of people
     one is unable to get what one wants in the world.
Therefore
     in auspicious matters the left is in highest regard,
     in matters of mourning the right is in highest regard.
Therefore
     the lieutenant general stands to the left
     and the supreme commander stands to the right.
That is to say:
     they are positioned in accordance with funeral rites.
When masses of people are killed,
     this is faced with grief and sorrow.
When a war is won,
     the occasion is treated with funeral rites.

Commentary on Chapter Thirty-two

This chapter intertwines a number of Daoist notions and images. It states that the Dao is without name and this namelessness is then associated with the "uncarved wood." Wood that is yet uncarved does not yet have a function; it has not yet taken on a specific shape. That which has a shape, accordingly, has a name, but that which precedes shape and is still shapeless is unnamed. The uncarved wood represents the shapelessness of the Dao—or, to put it in positive terms, its ultimate potentiality—that corresponds to its namelessness.

The Dao is then put in the context of the exertion of political power. That which has no name has no function, and consequently it is not subordinated to anything. A name in the social context designates a specific role in society, an office, or a duty. That which has no name is not in a particular service. Namelessness therefore corresponds to rulership. The ruler who rules according to the Dao acts through nonaction and this leads to a "self-so" (*ziran*) or natural subordination of the people. Such a ruler will not be coercive, or, as chapter 17 states, people will only know that he exists. Thus they will accept such a ruler unconditionally. In such a society, heaven and earth will "give sweet dew," which is to say that nature will be in harmony with society and life will be fertile and productive.

Towards the end of chapter the "mastery of cessation" or of "knowing when to stop" (*zhi zhi*) is mentioned. This is a crucial Daoist skill. The "mastery of cessation" is the art of evading indulgence, longing, and addiction.

The last lines are rather disconnected from the rest of the chapter. Here, the imagery of water is reintroduced. The Dao is equated with that body of water which lies lowest and towards which all others effortlessly flow. And, as the pivot of fertility, it is from this low-lying water that life emerges. The Dao is thus compared with the ocean.

Thirty-two

三十二

The Dao is constantly without name.
Although the uncarved wood is only small,
      the world does not dare to regard it as subordinate.

If marquises and kings can maintain it,
      then the ten thousand things submit to them by
         themselves.
Heaven and earth combine
      to give sweet dew.
Without orders being issued, the people will by themselves
   enter into an equilibrium.

When the carving is begun,
      then there are names.
When there are names
      then one will also master cessation.
The mastery of cessation
      is that by which one remains without danger.

In comparison, the Dao is to the world
      what rivers and oceans are to small valleys.

Commentary on Chapter Thirty-three

The previous chapter mentioned the "mastery of cessation" or "knowing when to stop" (*zhi zhi*). This chapter recalls this phrase by speaking about "knowing when it is enough" or the "mastery of satisfaction" (*zhi zu*). One who knows when to stop, and therefore knows when there is enough, has mastered the art of satisfaction. The mastery of cessation and the mastery of satisfaction are the same. To be content or "rich" does not depend on the quantity of one's possessions, but on the ability to feel satisfied with what one has. Satisfaction is not measured by what one owns but by the absence of unfulfilled wishes.

The overcoming of oneself is immediately connected with the art of satisfaction. This art is the overcoming of the yearnings and cravings of one's ego. The concepts of knowing and overcoming are paralleled in the first lines of this chapter. Their meaning is related even in English when one considers that "to master" can mean both "to know (how)" and "to dominate."[5] To gain control of oneself is even more difficult than controlling others, and if one is able to master oneself—in the double meaning of the word—then one will truly know how to live a life of contentment.

I translated the last line of this chapter according to the Mawangdui version of the text. Wang Bi's version has "does not perish" instead of "is not forgotten." The Mawangdui version is more Confucian in tone. In Confucianism, to be remembered after one's death was highly important and ancient ancestral rites served exactly this function. It was believed that the spirits of ancestors could persist as long as the rituals that kept them in contact with their living descendants were continued.

---

5. See Wittgenstein, *Philosophische Untersuchungen*, 315 (paragraph 150).

Thirty-three

三十三

The one who knows others is knowledgeable.
    To know oneself is clarity.
The one who overcomes others has force.
    To overcome oneself is to be strong.

The one who knows when it is enough is rich.
The one who acts out of strength has a will.
The one who does not lose his place is long lasting.
The one who dies but is not forgotten has longevity.

Commentary on Chapter Thirty-four

Many chapters in the *Laozi* speak about the Dao in terms of water. Here, it is compared to the motion of water, the flowing or drifting that moves into any direction. The flow of water is the most "natural" movement. It is always perfectly adapted to its environment and moves effortlessly. The movement of the Dao also happens without any effort or "driving force" that tries to impose a certain direction. Nature and water move "self-so" (*ziran*).

The second and third stanzas of this chapter relate the "action" of the sage—and the sage ruler—to the effortless motion of the Dao. The Dao does not act as a ruler because it is without desire. It has no intention to force anything on nature. This absence of a particular intention or specific function leaves it without a name that would identify it with an exclusive role. Therefore it is, on the one hand, the smallest of all—it is empty of all positive features, like water it is bland and shapeless. On the other hand, in accordance with the paradoxical logic of Daoism, the very absence of particular qualities makes the Dao, like water, also "great" because all things depend on it. All life depends on the nourishing qualities of water and everything in nature follows the "great" Dao. The sage ruler follows this model and minimizes his personal intentions and willful actions. By not acting on the course of nature he allows the way of nature or the Dao to proceed unimpeded.

Thirty-four

三十四

The Dao—
>How it flows!
>Left and right it can be.

The task is completed,
the duty is fulfilled,
>but it is without name.
The ten thousand things return to it,
>but it does not act as their ruler,
>so that it is constantly without desire.
It can be named with the small.
The ten thousand things return to it,
>but it does not act as their ruler.
It can be mandated with the great.

Therefore
>the sage can accomplish the great
>by his not acting on the great.
Thus he can accomplish the great.

Commentary on Chapter Thirty-five

The "great image" is mostly interpreted (as early as in the Heshang Gong commentary) as the Dao. In the *Yijing*, or *Book of Changes*, the term for "image" (*xiang*) is of particular importance. It designates, among other things, the four primary constellations of Yin and Yang that constitute the semiotic pattern of this ancient Chinese oracular classic and thus the cosmological order. The "Great Commentary" to the *Yijing* states famously: "One Yin, one Yang: this is called Dao."[6] The "great image" is the Dao as the rhythm of Yin and Yang or the pulse of the world—here one may be reminded of the image of the bellows in chapter 5. The first lines seem to be addressed to the sage ruler and imply that he is in harmony with that rhythm, then the people will naturally follow him and the society will be orderly and peaceful.

The second stanza reads like a saying. Where there is a festivity, passers-by will remain. Perhaps this is meant to resonate with the first stanza. Just as people flock to a place where music is played and a feast is served, they will naturally rally around the ruler who is in accord with the cosmic rhythm of the Dao.

The last stanza is explicitly introduced as a saying about the Dao. Its nonqualities are once more praised. It is without a specific taste, shape, or sound, and yet—or, rather, because of this—use does not wear it down . To use the imagery of chapter 11, it is like a door, a pot, or a wheel, its emptiness guarantees its inexhaustible functionality.

---

6. *Dazhuan* (or: *Xici*), chapter 2.

Thirty-five

三十五

Hold the great image,
  and the world comes.
It comes without harm.
Peacefulness and tranquility are great.

Where there is music and feasting—
  one passes by, one goes there, one stops.

Thus, about the Dao there is a saying brought forth:
How bland—it is without taste!
Looking at it
  does not suffice to see it.
Listening to it
  does not suffice to hear it.
Using it
  cannot exhaust it.

Commentary on Chapter Thirty-six

If you want to be successful, this chapter states, you have to master the strategy of the paradox. The art of government and the means of taking and holding on to power are based on the ability to conform to the paradoxical functioning of the Dao. That which is overextended will eventually collapse into itself. That which becomes too strong will, in the long run, weaken itself. In politics, one can only leave and weaken those whom one has earlier joined and strengthened—and those whom you want to dominate must be given presents and favors. This seems to be the message here, and the first part of the chapter was interpreted in this strategic way by Hanfeizi. Even if these rules are not used to overcome others, it is important to be aware of them so that they are not effective against you.

The mastery of this strategy of the paradox results in having "sublime clarity" about the workings of the Dao. The most basic rule of reversal is that the weak and the soft will eventually overcome the strong and the hard (see chapters 76 and 78).

Another strategic maxim is not to expose oneself. This is like taking a fish out of the water and it will inevitably lead to failure and ruin. The ruler who displays himself openly will thereby weaken himself (see chapter 24). Similarly, the exposure of weapons should be avoided. This will only lead to militarization and possibly war (see chapters 31, 68, 69, and 80). The strategies for winning a war—such as the maxims mentioned in the first stanza—are only to be made use of when a war cannot be avoided. The preferable option is not to have one in the first place.

Thirty-six

三十六

What you intend to shrink
    you should make sure to stretch.
What you intend to weaken
    you should make sure to strengthen.
What you intend to leave
    you should make sure to join.
What you intend to snatch
    you should make sure to bestow upon.

This is called: subtle clarity.
The soft and weak defeats the strong.

Fish are not to be taken out of the depths.
In the state, sharp tools are not to be exposed to the people.

Commentary on Chapter Thirty-seven

This chapter connects to the themes addressed in chapter 32 and even repeats some of the same verses. The Dao is without positive qualities, and if the sage ruler rules in accord with it, that is, with perfect impartiality and without taking action, then the people will follow him without feeling forced. The "uncarved wood"—which is also mentioned in chapter 32—is used as an image of the art of rulership. The uncarved wood symbolizes the unlimited potentiality of the Dao that has not yet taken on form. It is through this power that the ruler rules, and if anybody in the state attempts to act against the course of the Dao, they will be subdued. The first line in the *Huang-Lao Boshu*, a text ascribed to the school of so-called Huang-Lao Daoism and excavated along with the Mawangdui manuscripts of the *Laozi*, states: "The Dao generates the law [*fa*]." This sentence may be understood in conjunction with what this chapter says. The ruler's standards originate in the Dao. If anything violates its natural role, the ruler will restrain it. In this way there is "tranquility" in society and in heaven and on earth, which is also to say that nature will naturally be in order.

Thirty-seven

三十七

The Dao is constantly without name.
> If marquises and kings can maintain it
> then the ten thousand things change by themselves.
That which changes and then desires to take action
> I will subdue with the nameless, uncarved wood.
> If it is subdued with the nameless, uncarved wood,
> only then will it be blameless.
By being blameless,
> there will be tranquility.
Heaven and earth will be correct by themselves.

Commentary on Chapter Thirty-eight

This is the first chapter of the second section of the Dao-*De*-Jing. The order of the two sections is reversed in the Mawangdui manuscripts so that there it is the first chapter of the first section. Obviously, it is about *de* and the whole section was later entitled *De*—which is why the book was called the Dao-De-Jing, that is, the Classic (*jing*) of Dao and De.

The first three stanzas echo chapter 18 and present a critique of the Confucian "cardinal virtues," particularly of *de*. In the Confucian context it is best translated as "virtue," whereas I normally translate it in the context of the *Laozi* as "efficacy." For the Confucians, *de* had a strong moral connotation and was associated with concepts such as humanity (*ren*), righteousness (*yi*), and ritual propriety (*li*). In the context of the *Laozi*, *de* is stripped of this moral connotation and is more closely associated with the Dao. Here, it is the "efficacy" that goes along with the Dao. Higher "virtue" is thus, as the first line says, not *de* in the Confucian moral sense. True virtue is beyond virtue and is not moral—it becomes pure efficacy. Virtue that clings to Confucian values is powerless from the perspective of the *Laozi*. The chapter, then, like chapter 18, goes on to portray the Confucian sequence of values as a downward spiral. Once a moral way of looking at life is established, the road towards forceful action is begun and a return to the natural self-so (*ziran*) of the cosmic order becomes ever more difficult.

The last two stanzas are usually understood as mutually explanatory. The last stanza clearly implies that the "great man" will not stick to ritual propriety and foreknowledge. The concept of "foreknowledge" would thus be something negative. The Heshang Gong commentary notes that this means inadequate and pretended knowledge that misses the substance or the "fruit" and remains only on the surface or on the level of the "flower" of the Dao. This interpretation of "foreknowledge" is well founded within the context of this chapter, but it becomes a little dubious when read in conjunction with other chapters. The "simplemindedness" (*yu*) that is mentioned is, in two other chapters (10 and 65), not negative, but rather something positive. To be in accord with the Dao is often depicted as being without any particular knowledge and thus in possession of the ability to intuitively follow the course of things. Read in this context, the verse about foreknowledge may be read as yet more praise for intellectual simplicity. Foreknowledge would then be the intuitive insight into the course of the Dao.

Thirty-eight

三十八

Higher virtue [de] is not virtuous [de],
    therefore it has efficacy [de].
Lower virtue does not let go of virtue,
    therefore it has no efficacy.

Higher virtue does not act and has no purpose.
Higher humanity acts and has no purpose.
Higher righteousness acts and has a purpose.
Higher ritual propriety acts and nothing resonates with it
    so that the sleeves are rolled up and coercion is exerted.

Thus,
After the Dao is lost there is virtue.
After virtue is lost there is humanity.
After humanity is lost there is righteousness.
After righteousness is lost there is ritual propriety.

Well,
Ritual propriety is the thin type of loyalty and trustworthiness
    and the beginning of disorder.
Foreknowledge is the flowering of the Dao
    and the beginning of being simpleminded.

Therefore the great man
    resides with the thick and does not reside with the thin,
    resides with the fruit and not with the flower.
Thus he discards that and picks this.

Commentary on Chapter Thirty-nine

As a numerical symbol, "one" or "oneness" stands for the Dao. The oneness of the Dao provides for the integration of the realms of heaven, earth, and society—which includes the realm of the "spirits." This resonates with chapter 25, which also speaks of the Dao as the embracing pattern that unites these areas. The second stanza probably means to say that all these realms function the way they do only because they are integrated into the pattern of the Dao—and because they follow the Daoist rule of the paradox. This is particularly the case with the valley whose emptiness allows for things to grow (see chapter 6). Similarly, and this is what the following lines seem to say, the political rulers use depreciatory terms to designate themselves (the "orphaned," the "abandoned," and the "one without possessions" were actual self-designations of rulers in ancient China) in order to declare their emptiness—a lack of social bonds (which would make them partial to their kinsmen at the expense of others) and of personal property (since this would tie them to what they own). Only by being "empty" can the ruler manifest the Dao and thus qualify for being the regent in the first place. It is this paradoxical rule of reversal, which turns the lowest into the highest, that their position is based upon. The last lines state once more that the Daoist ruler does not display himself and that he identifies his rulership with the soft (and female), and not with the hard (and male).

Thirty-nine

三十九

Of those who once received oneness:
     heaven received oneness—to be clear;
     earth received oneness—to be at rest;
     spirits received oneness—to be animated;
     valleys received oneness—to be full;
     lords and kings received oneness—to set the world straight.

This leads to saying:
Heaven is not to be already clear,
     lest it may shatter.
Earth is not to be already at rest,
     lest it may burst.
Spirits are not to be already animated,
     lest they may wear out.
River valleys are not to be already full,
     lest they may be exhausted.
Marquises and kings are not to be already esteemed and of
   high standing
     lest they may stumble.

Thus,
     necessarily the noble has the base as its root,
     necessarily the high has the low as its foundation.
Well, therefore
     lords and kings call themselves the "orphaned," the
        "abandoned," and the "one without possessions."
It is in this way that they root themselves in the base, isn't it?
For this reason they do not desire
     to be shining like jade,
     to be hard like stone.

Commentary on Chapter Forty

This chapter is one of the shortest in the *Daodejing*, but also one of the best known and philosophically most important. The reversal mentioned here pertains to the circular movement of the course of Dao. As chapter 25 points out, with such movement progress is at the same time a return to the beginning. The same circular movement is apparent in the course of the four seasons and of the heavenly bodies in the sky. Similarly, day turns into night, and life turns into death. The reversal of the Dao is also present in the strategies of the paradox. That which moves to the fore will be defeated and that which stays hidden will lead. Reversal is also the movement of the wheel (that is mentioned in chapter 11) whose motion consists in the constant turning of the spokes.

The second line is one specific application of this rule of reversal. That which is weak (and soft) will eventually overcome that which is strong (and hard). The image of weakness (and softness) is one of the main images in Daoism and associated with the qualities of the female. The triumph of the weak, soft, and feminine over the strong, hard, and masculine exemplifies the Daoist paradox.

The next verse, which is as terse and concise as the first one, can be read in conjunction with chapter 42. The Dao that is empty and without form and name is nonpresent. This generates that which is present, that is, the realm of the ten thousand things. As I will point out in the commentary to chapter 42, this scenario of generation does not necessarily have to be read as a "history" of being. It does not necessary mean that the Dao precedes the world in time. It rather means that the Dao, just like the root of a plant, is the element of generation within a circle of production and reproduction. That which generates the generated is itself part of the monistic circle of generation.

Forty

四十

Reversal is the movement of the Dao.
Weakness is the usefulness of the Dao.

The things of the world are generated from presence (*you*).
Presence is generated from nonpresence (*wu*).

Commentary on Chapter Forty-one

The first stanza introduces a "ranking" of human dealings with the Dao that is reminiscent of the ranking of rulers in chapter 17. And these lines may well also be addressed to rulers. The worst kind of ruler is ridiculed by the people—and he himself can only laugh at the Dao he does not understand. The best kind of ruler, of course, practices the Dao. The reason for the difficulty of grasping and practicing the Dao is connected with what the second stanza describes: the workings of the Dao and its efficacy are paradoxical. As is described in the preceding chapter and chapter 25, the course of the Dao is one of reversal. Similarly, for instance, in order to lead the people, the ruler has to step back (see chapter 7). To retreat means to lead. The last stanza in this chapter also seems to allude to such a course where beginning and end overlap. The end of one cycle is the beginning of the next. A proper end is also a good place for a beginning—such is the seamless course of time. If, for instance, a season ends at the proper time then the next season begins at the right time.

This chapter also includes a number of images and characterizations that are typical for the *Laozi* and for Daoism in general. The Dao is said to be dark (see chapter 1), efficacy (*de*) is associated with the river valley (see chapter 6), and formlessness as well as namelessness and "silent tones" (see chapter 23) are paradigmatic features of the Dao.

Forty-one

四十一

When the higher kind of people hear of the Dao,
    they can, with diligence, practice it.
When average people hear of the Dao,
    it will, in part, be realized, and, in part, it will be lost.
When the lower kind of people hear of the Dao,
    they will laugh at it,
    and if they would not laugh at it, it would not suffice to
      be the Dao.

Therefore there is an established saying that goes:
    The bright Dao resembles darkness.
    The advancing Dao resembles going back.
    The smooth Dao resembles the uneven.
    Higher efficacy resembles the river valley.
    The great white resembles the sullied.
    Vast efficacy resembles the insufficient.
    Solid efficacy resembles the infirm.
    Thorough genuineness resembles variation.

The great square has no corners.
The great vessel is late completed.
The great sound has silent tones.
The great image has no form.

The Dao is lofty and without name.
Well, the Dao alone
    is good for the beginning
    and also good for the completion.

Commentary on Chapter Forty-two

The first and second stanzas of this chapter resonate with chapter 40 and should be read in conjunction with it. What is said in chapter 40 in conceptual terms is here expressed through numerical symbols. Chapter 40 stated: "The things of the world are generated from presence (*you*). Presence is generated from nonpresence (*wu*)." Chapter 42 states, in the reverse order, that one generates two, two generates three, and so on. At the center of the process of generation is the Dao which is identified with nothingness (*wu*) or emptiness as well as with the number one (note: not zero) that stands for both singleness and totality. Explained with the help of the image of the wheel, the Dao is both the empty and single hub (the inward center and "origin" of the wheel's function) as well as the whole wheel (the outward totality of all that happens or the monistic cosmos). As mentioned in the commentary to chapter 35, the *Book of Changes* states: "One Yin, one Yang: this is called Dao."[7] The whole scenario of the Dao consists of the rhythm of Yin and Yang, of night and day, darkness and brightness, or, in the world of the biological, of female and male. The course of production and reproduction is based on this most general duality. Thus, the monistic whole encompasses "twoness." This oneness and twoness together constitute the threeness that stands for the multiplicity of the ten thousand things. Seen as a totality, the Dao is one, but its oneness is just the frame of a fundamental twoness that is at the heart of change and reproduction. This duality, in turn, gives rise to all there is in the world. The whole process of generation that is described here in numerical symbols should not be understood as a genesis or a linear evolution, but rather as, like in the image of the wheel, an integrated cycle. The movement of the wheel revolves around the empty hub at the center, but the hub does not precede or initiate the turning of the wheel. The Dao is not a first mover or creator; it is at the center of a process of production and reproduction.

---

7. *Dazhuan* (or: *Xici*), chapter 2.

The chapter continues with a series of four rather unrelated sayings. The third stanza repeats in slight variation a line from chapter 39. The fourth stanza resonates with the topic of chapter 48—to exercise the Dao means, in paradoxical fashion, to gain by loss. The fifth stanza sounds quite Confucian and is more or less self-explanatory. The last stanza reintroduces the idea that the application of force will, again following the rule of the paradox, result not in domination but in defeat.

Forty-two

四十二

The Dao generates Oneness.
Oneness generates Twoness.
Twoness generates Threeness.
Threeness generates the ten thousand things.

The ten thousand things;
      carrying Yin, embracing Yang—
      blending Qi to create harmony.

What the world hates,
      is to be orphaned, abandoned, and without possession
and still kings and lords name therewith themselves.

As to things,
      in part they are added to by diminishment
      or diminished by addition.

Thus,
that which one has been taught with
one also considers when teaching others.

Thus the saying
      "The coercive and violent does not meet his natural end"
shall be the father of my teaching.

Commentary on Chapter Forty-three

This chapter begins with a saying that is formulated as a riddle, a manner of speaking that is typical of the *Laozi* and oral literature in general. The "very softest" has been traditionally, and in connection with chapter 78, interpreted as water, and the "very hardest" is the stone or rock that it runs over. That which has "no presence" (*wu you*) has been interpreted as the Dao—an interpretation that I prefer and that is supported by the Heshang Gong commentary. Alternatively, Wang Bi and others have taken it to mean the universal "medium" or "energy" called Qi, which is mentioned in the preceding chapter. One could here also translate *wu you* concretely as "no fullness"—and that which has no fullness and is empty is, obviously, the Dao.

The second stanza connects the previous one to the art of government. The "I" is again the "I" of the prospective reader or listener who is, of course, the sage ruler. Once the riddle of the first stanza is solved, the paradoxical functioning of water and the Dao is clear, which allows for insight into the strategy of reversal: Nonacting is the superior way of acting and the most beneficial form of governance.

The last stanza links the maxim of nonaction to the "teaching of nonspeaking." Since nonaction (*wu wei*) and nonspeaking (*bu yan*) go together, nonspeaking does *not* lead to a total abstinence from language. Nonaction (on behalf of the ruler) is the basis for perfect action (on behalf of the people). Similarly, it can be inferred that "nonspeaking," or the absence of explicitly or implicitly taking sides, is not meant to suppress all language, but to allow for its unimpeded functioning. The ruler does not himself take action or engage in debates. It is this noninterference and impartiality that allows actions and language to unfold harmoniously.

Forty-three

四十三

The very softest in the world
    runs quickly over the very hardest in the world.
That which has no presence
    penetrates that which has no interstice.

Therefore I know about
    the benefit of nonaction.

The teaching of nonspeaking,
the benefit of nonaction:
    few in the world can get there.

Commentary on Chapter Forty-four

The Heshang Gong commentary characterizes the three stanzas of this chapter as "warnings," and this is obviously what they are. The first stanza warns that a concern for fame and wealth may well cost one one's body. The recipe for both physical and mental health, that is, the absence of sickness and worry, is not to strive for material goods or official positions. The second stanza continues in the same vein when it says that emotional and material expenditures are to be avoided. Both emotional and material investments will eventually lead to loss and harm one's well-being. The last stanza summarizes the Daoist message of this chapter. The "mastery of cessation" (*zhi zhi*, see also chapter 32 for this expression) will lead to satisfaction and health. Knowing when one has had enough is the basis for contentment.

Forty-four

四十四

Reputation or body—what is closer?
Body or property—what is more?
To get or to lose—what is more distressing?

Where there is deep sympathy,
    there is great expenditure.
Where there is much stored,
    there will be heavy loss.

Thus,
To know when it is enough is to be without disgrace.
To master cessation is to be without peril.
Long duration becomes possible.

Commentary on Chapter Forty-five

The first stanza resonates with other parts of the *Laozi* (such as chapters 6 and 11) that praise the inexhaustible quality of the empty. That which is perfectly usable without any "wear or tear" has emptiness as its main function. Here one may recall the pot and the doors and windows of chapter 11. The second stanza resonates with the lines in chapter 25 that state: "Greatness means to proceed. / To proceed means distance. / Distance means return." The "great" line is that of the circle which returns to its beginning. Although it appears that time and space unfold linearly, the Dao, as the great cosmic scenario, is "bent." It is a cycle of production, reproduction, and return. Similarly paradoxical is the skill of the sage. It is a nonskill that seems to be clumsy. By not being trained in any specific function, the sage (ruler) is the only one who remains inactive and thereby takes on the position at the heart of all the specific activities. The greatest craftsperson does not master any specific craft, and it is in this nonpossession of any specific traits or goods that being greatly gifted consists.

The final stanza praises the qualities of stillness and tranquility that are often associated with the Dao (see also chapters 16, 37, 57, and 61) and the Daoist maxim of nonaction. The last line puts the "negative" qualities of stillness and tranquility once more in a social or political context by addressing the art of rulership.

Forty-five

四十五

Great completion resembles a vacancy,
    in its use it is not worn out.
The greatly filled resembles emptiness,
    in its use it is not exhausted.

Great straightness is as if bent.
Great skill is as if clumsy.
Great profit is as if lacking.

Activity defeats cold.
Stillness defeats heat.
Tranquil and still—
    therewith the world can be adjusted.

Commentary on Chapter Forty-six

This chapter addresses desires and their disadvantages. The first stanza compares two different states of society. When the Dao prevails, no one has the desire to go anywhere (compare with chapter 80) because they are content. Horses are then used for agriculture and not travel. When the Dao does not prevail, the breeding of horses is a matter of warfare. This is a state in which emotions are unrestrained and desire reigns—it is a state of unfulfilled want. The second stanza directly relates to the first and points out that a ruler has to make sure that such a state of desire and want does not arise. Desires arise when people do not know that they have enough and thirst for more. Such a state of want is the cause of war, social disorder, and strife. The desire to acquire is the core reason for political unrest and the competition between countries or societies. The last stanza explains that satisfaction has nothing to do with the amount of possessions but with the ability to be satisfied with what is enough (see chapters 32, 33, and 44). If one does not master this art, one will always crave more. There is no limit to the cycle of addiction that occurs in such states of desire. Only satisfaction that arises from the mastery of cessation can be lasting.

Forty-six

四十六

When the world has the Dao,
      saddle-horses are returned to fertilize the fields.
When the world does not have the Dao,
      war horses are bred in the outskirts.

Of crimes, none is greater
      than to allow for desires.
Of disasters, none is greater
      than not to master satisfaction.
Of calamities, none is sadder
      than the desire to acquire.

Thus,
      the satisfaction of the mastery of satisfaction
      is constant satisfaction.

Commentary on Chapter Forty-seven

This is one of the most famous explications of the maxim "doing nothing and nothing is undone" (*wu wei er wu bu wei*). It is surprisingly similar to two passages in the *Analects* of Confucius that read: "The Master said: 'The one who brought about order by nonaction—was this not Shun!? And what did he do? He simply assumed an air of deference and faced due south'" (section 15.5[8]) and "The Master said: 'Governing with efficacy can be compared to being the North Star: the North Star dwells in its place, and the multitude of stars pay tribute'" (section 2.1[9]). By remaining still at the center of the cosmic and political scenario the sage ruler gives order to nature and the state just like the hub does to the wheel. He is, at the same time, ascribed knowledge of "the Dao of heaven." As was noted earlier with respect to chapter 33, "to know" can also mean "to master." By keeping his position, the ruler knows *how* to govern the world. It is, in paradoxical fashion, precisely because he remains unmoved at the center that the sage ruler demonstrates that he has this "know-how" of the cosmos and society. If he left his position he would not gain more knowledge but show that he does not have a true understanding of rulership. The ruler is able to stabilize society from within and he can even "name" correctly, that is, assign the proper functions in the state, without leaving his place.

---

8. See the translation by Ames and Rosemont, *Analects of Confucius*, 185 (translation modified).

9. Ames and Rosemont, *Analects of Confucius*, 76 (translation modified).

Forty-seven

四十七

Not to go out of the door—
    to know the world.
Not to look out of the window—
    to know the Dao of heaven.

The further one goes out,
    the less one will know.

Therefore the sage
    knows without going,
    names without seeing,
    completes without acting.

Commentary on Chapter Forty-eight

This chapter continues the central Daoist topic of *wu wei* (doing nothing, or nonaction) that was taken up in the preceding chapter. Practicing the Dao does not mean, as it does for some Confucians, an increase in learning and "knowing-that." It rather means a self-minimization. The perfect sage has to empty himself of thoughts, words, and actions. That the *Laozi* looks at this practice from a political perspective becomes obvious in the last stanza of the chapter. *Wu wei* is the practice of the sage ruler. Since the sage ruler is the only person who does not take on any specific function in the state—since he does not become a spoke within the wheel of society—he remains the only one who is qualified to take on the position of leadership—namely, the hub of the social wheel. If he took on a specific duty he would no longer be in the proper position to lead. This nonaction on his behalf is, as the chapter clearly states, the precondition for all duties being fulfilled and all actions being harmoniously performed (by others). By doing nothing the sage ruler ensures that nothing remains undone in his country.

Forty-eight

四十八

One who engages in learning
    increases daily.
One who hears of the Dao
    diminishes daily.

To decrease and to decrease even more
    so that "doing nothing" [*wu wei*] is reached.
Doing nothing, and nothing is undone.

If one wants to take hold of the world
    one has to stay constantly without duty.
As soon as one has a duty,
    one in turn is not sufficient to take on the world.

Commentary on Chapter Forty-nine

The topic of this chapter is the "heartlessness" of the Daoist sage ruler. This personal heartlessness, however, means that he, at the center of society, *is* the heart of society. The ruler takes on the position in the state that the heart has in the body. He is the central organ, so to speak, and thus his heart has to be empty of personal feelings, thoughts, and intentions. In this way, no one has less "personality" than the sage ruler. This "dehumanization" of the sage goes along with his total impartiality. The sage does not distinguish between good and bad because he has no personal inclinations. Being at the hub of the social wheel, the ruler's perspective on everything around him is the same. The distinctions between the spokes are, from this perspective, not distinctions between "up" and "down" or "good" and "bad." The image of the wheel can also be used to explain the last stanza of this chapter. The sage ruler is at the center of society and merges his heart with the hearts of society as a whole. This makes all the people face him just as all the spokes of the wheel face the hub. The people "fix ears and eyes on him" and in this way they are united in a single community. It is through the centrality and impartiality of the sage that he can view all his subjects as "children." No one has a more or less privileged position. The sage ruler's indifference, his "heartlessness," enables him to treat every member of the community with perfect equanimity.

Forty-nine

四十九

The sage is constantly without a heart;
     he takes the heart of the common people as the heart.

That which is good
     he holds to be good.
That which is not good
     he also holds to be good.
Thus he attains goodness.
That which is true
     he holds to be true.
That which is not true
     he also holds to be true.
Thus he attains truth.

When the sage resides in the world,
       he fuses himself with it.
For the world he merges hearts.
All the people fix ears and eyes on him,
       and the sage regards them as smiling children.

Commentary on Chapter Fifty

The first sentence introduces the topic of this chapter: life and death. Once more, the Daoist rule of reversal comes into play. To live life means, at the same time, to die, or, to approach death. The movement of life can also be thought of as circular. By living life one moves toward the state that is before life.

The second stanza can be read as a riddle. The reader or listener is left to wonder what these "thirteen" are. Since antiquity, commentators have suggested different solutions. Wang Bi, for instance, reads "one third" instead of "thirteen." This is possible in his edition, but the choice is not well supported by the Mawangdui texts. Hanfeizi, the early Legalist commentator of the *Laozi*, interprets the "thirteen" as the four human limbs and the nine openings of the body. Read in this fashion, humans are able to live by the fact that the limbs move and there are openings through which one can expel and take things in. At the same time, the limbs create friction and lead towards death just as the openings inevitably leak energy. In the *Zhuangzi*, for instance, the legendary Hundun dies because some well-wishing visitors drill the seven openings into his face and thereby humanize him or bring him to life.[10] If read in this way, the riddle is an explanation of the first two verses.

The organs of life are also organs of death because they make the organism open and vulnerable. If an organism is able to close off all openings, it will have no place where it can be harmed—and this is what the third stanza declares. Thus the preservation of life consists in the minimization of points of friction.

---

10. This story concludes the seventh and last of the Inner Chapters of the *Zhuangzi*.

Fifty

五十

Going out into life.
Going in into death.

The companions of life are thirteen.
The companions of death are thirteen.
For the human beings moving on living their lives
      they all become thirteen spots of approaching death.
And for what reason?
      Because they live life.

It is heard of those who are good at holding on to life:
When they walk in the hills,
      they avoid neither rhinos nor tigers.
When they go into battle,
      they carry no armor or weapons.
The rhino has no spot to jab its horn.
The tiger has no spot to put its claws.
For weapons there is no spot to lodge a blade.
And for what reason?
Because they have no spots of death.

Commentary on Chapter Fifty-one

This chapter describes the relation between Dao and De and the "ten thousand things" (*wan wu*). Dao and De ("the way and its efficacy") are portrayed as that which not only "generates" (*sheng*) but also rears and nourishes all things. It is obvious that Dao and De are not creators in the strict sense of the word, but are rather, like the root of a plant, that "force" within the cosmos that sustains all there is. Dao and De are not separated from the ten thousand things; they are what "accompanies" them. The vocabulary used in this chapter to describe their function is related to agriculture and the raising of one's offspring. The cosmos is conceived of in terms of biological reproduction and fertility; it is understood as an "organic" process of life. Dao and De are integral elements within that process and not an external origin. The Daoist worldview is monistic, not dualistic. Within the cycle of generation and regeneration, Dao and De do not coerce the ten thousand things. What grows does so on its own. The ten thousand things "repay" the noncoercive and noninterfering nourishment of Dao and De by following what is natural to them. The response of the things consists simply in them being "self-so" (*ziran*).

Fifty-one

五十一

The Dao generates them;
De [efficacy] nourishes them;
As things they are formed;
And as utensils they are completed.

Therefore
      the ten thousand things honor the Dao
      and cherish the De [efficacy].
Honoring the Dao,
cherishing the De:
      none is rewarded for this,
      so it happens constantly "self-so."

The Dao generates them,
      nourishes them,
      lets them grow,
      accompanies them,
      rests them,
      secures them,
      fosters them,
      protects them.

Generating without possessing,
Acting without depending,
Rearing without ordaining:
This is called dark efficacy.

Commentary on Chapter Fifty-two

This chapter—at least at the beginning—continues the theme of the preceding one: The relation between the Dao and the world is one of generation and nourishment. The Dao is here presented as the "mother." It should again be stressed that the mother is not something external to the process of production and reproduction; but an integral moment within it. Mother and children coexist in one world, and the children depend on the mother for their nourishment. The mother is that element within a process of reproduction that has the power to give life; it is the source of fertility in an "organic" cosmos. The mother can be "returned" to—and this is to say that reproduction is cyclical. If one looks at the course of life as such a cyclical movement (like the life of plants which, in winter, "return" to their root and then, in the spring, grow anew) one understands that while individuals may die, the whole process of change from life to death never ends. There is always a return to the beginning and thus the beginning renews itself continuously. The beginning is integrated into a course of change, not some ultimate starting point that precedes the unfolding of time. As the last lines states, the Dao is associated with permanence, and this is different, for instance, from Christian notions of eternity which conceive of a dimension of the divine that is beyond mundane temporality. The Dao, unlike God, is thoroughly within the continuous, reproductive process of change—it is this very process. It is more like "mother nature" than God the father.

The second and third stanzas refer to bodily openings as a source of death. Energy "leaks out" of these openings. Daoist bodily cultivation therefore aims at closing them. Another source of friction is activity. The Daoist sage avoids active engagement in order to keep the body unharmed.

Fifty-two

五十二

The world has a beginning:
    it is considered the mother of the world.
Get to the mother
    in order to know the sons.
Return to the mother and preserve her,
    be unendangered by the transitoriness of the body.

Fill the openings, close the entries,
    be unencumbered by the termination of the body.

Open up the openings, be busy with affairs,
    and you will not be saved from the termination of the
        body.

To see the small is called clarity.
To keep the weak is called strength.

Make use of its radiance,
return again to its clarity,
do not abandon the body to calamities.
This is called:
    following continuity.

Commentary on Chapter Fifty-three

This chapter begins by speaking in the first person. The "I" that is mentioned is not that of any author, it is rather the "I" that the reader or listener is supposed to identify with. The Dao is a smooth way—but because it is so smooth it may cause those who walk on it to look for more "exciting" alternatives. To take action and leave the smooth way for more arduous paths, however, will not lead to success.

The remaining parts of the chapter depict a state in disorder. A ruling elite that is obviously not in line with the Dao has gathered the wealth of the country and neglects the duties of government. They have more than enough food and rely on the sword to protect their position because the people are starving. Such rulers are compared to "robbers"—which, in Chinese, is also pronounced *dao*. The Dao of exploitative rulers is one of robbery, and not the true Dao.

Fifty-three

五十三

If I had ample knowledge
    and would walk on the great way [Dao],
      my only worry would be to go astray.
The great way is very level.
People greatly like mountain paths.

The court is very neglected.
The fields are very fallow.
The granaries are very empty.

The clothing is ornamented and colorful,
    there is a sharp sword on the girdle.
Satiated with food,
    there are more than enough goods and possessions.

This is called: "Robbery."
Robbery is not the Dao.

This chapter sounds very Confucian. The first stanza praises the un-interrupted continuity of the family—which is of prime importance for Confucians. As the Confucian philosopher Mencius (4A.26) famously stated: "There are three kinds of filial impiety. To produce no male heirs is the greatest." If a family had no male descendants, it had no one to continue the ancestral sacrifices and thus keep the ancestors alive. Not having a son would then extinguish the ancestors and put an end to the whole family. This is a different quest for permanence from what is typically found in the *Laozi* and other Daoist texts. For the Daoists, permanence is not tied to the family or the clan, but to the body, the state, or the cosmos. Nature, for instance, is perceived as a permanent cycle of life and death.

The second and third stanzas are very similar to the Confucian *Great Learning* (*Da Xue*) which was initially part of a ritual text. Later it gained the status of an independent "classic." The subject of both these lines and the *Great Learning* is the spread of a ruler's cultivation from his own person to the whole world. Both Daoism and Confucianism viewed the realms of the individual body, the social community, and nature as a whole as interconnected.

Fifty-four

五 十 四

That which is well established is not uprooted.
That which is well embraced does not escape.
The line of sons and grandsons to perform the sacrificial
    rituals is not interrupted.

When cultivation reaches the body,
        efficacy will be genuine.
When cultivation reaches the family,
        efficacy will be abundant.
When cultivation reaches the village community,
        efficacy will be lasting.
When cultivation reaches the state,
        efficacy will be rich.
When cultivation reaches the world,
        efficacy will be broad.

Watching the body on the basis of the body;
watching the family on the basis of the family;
watching the village community on the basis of the village
    community;
watching the state on the basis of the state;
watching the world on the basis of the world.

How do I know how the world is?
Thus.

The infant is an important image of the Daoist sage. The "return to the mother" of which chapter 52 speaks can be read as the aim of Daoist cultivation. One is supposed to return to a state of infancy or even to an embryonic state when one does not yet have any "openings" (see chapter 52) that can leak energy. The infant is depicted as invulnerable. Speaking in the language of chapter 50, the infant or the embryo has not yet begun to "live its life" and therefore it does not yet have "spots of death." This is why wild animals do not hurt it. At the same time the lack of openings or leaks ensures that the infant has an unlimited potential of energy—it can cry all day without tiring and its grip is firm. Similarly, it is not sexually active—it does not ejaculate—but its penis stays erect for a long time. These are examples of the "maximum of vital essence" that is maintained by not squandering or losing any power.

The "return to the mother" and to the state of infancy can be understood more or less literally as a prescription for bodily cultivation. Daoist practice could aim at "closing" one's body and retaining all energies within oneself (as, for instance, the sexual practice of avoiding ejaculation well demonstrates). It can also, however, be interpreted more "philosophically" as the return to a state before the emergence of self-consciousness. The infant or the embryo has not yet developed an "ego," it has no "free will," no morality, and does not yet distinguish between right and wrong. It is still an instinctive being that has preserved its "animal nature." It acts without acting and, what it does do happens "self-so" (*ziran*). At the fringes of life, the state of the infant is the least "human" phase in our life—and the most "natural." Daoist cultivation of the "heart-mind" aimed at a return to this preconscious state. This state is opposed to the state of "growing up and getting old" (see chapter 30 for a discussion of this phrase). Maintaining the natural state of the infant was conceived of as being in harmony with the Dao.

Fifty-five

五十五

One who embodies the fullness of efficacy [de]
    is like an infant.
Wasps, scorpions, vipers, and snakes
    do not bite it.
Birds of prey and wild beasts
    do not seize it.
Bones and muscles are soft and weak,
    but its grip is firm.

It does not know yet about the joining of the male and the
    female,
        but its penis is erect.
This is the maximum of vital essence.
It screams all day
    without getting hoarse.
This is the maximum of harmony.
To know harmony is called "permanence."
To know permanence is called "clarity."
To increase in life is called a "bad omen."
If the heart directs the Qi, this is called: "forcing."

If a thing grows up and then gets old,
    this is called "not the Dao."
"Not the Dao" ends early.

Commentary on Chapter Fifty-six

The topic of speechlessness occurs quite frequently in the *Laozi* (see chapters 2, 23, 43, and 73) and is connected with nonaction. The sage ruler does not act and thereby allows all actions to be performed without interference. Similarly, the sage ruler does not speak; he does not personally give any orders. This gives rise to a state in which all speech, that is, orders, assignments, and so on, happens "self-so" (*ziran*), as chapter 23 puts it. The speechlessness of the sage ruler also corresponds to the namelessness of the Dao. Just as the namelessness of the Dao does not mean that there are no names in the world (see chapter 1), the speechlessness of the sage ruler does not mean that there is no speech in society. The nameless Dao is the anchor of all the named and the speechless sage ruler is the center of all speech in society. It should also be noted once more (see chapter 33) that "to know" means "to know how" or "to master." The sage ruler who has the "know-how" of government will not speak (just as he will not act) while the ruler who lacks this will, on the contrary, attempt to order the state with his own deeds and words. This will lead to disorder.

The second stanza refers once more to the topic of the "blocking of openings" (see chapters 50 and 52). In rather "dark" language it advises one to be spare and to avoid friction and the leaking of energy.

The last stanza may again be read in a political context. The sage ruler will not develop any "special relationships." Like the hub within a wheel that has the same relation to all spokes, the ruler is completely impartial. One can neither befriend (he does not, for instance, receive gifts or favors; see chapter 13) nor alienate him. It is this "indifference" that makes the sage ruler so prestigious and guarantees him the respect of the people.

Fifty-six

五十六

One who knows does not speak.
One who speaks does not know.

Blocking the holes,
    closing the gates;
softening the radiance,
    leveling the dust;
grinding the sharp,
    untying the tangles;
this is called: "dark unity."

Thus,
one cannot get him and make him one's kin,
    and one cannot get him and keep him distant;
one cannot get him and let him profit,
    and one cannot get him and do him harm;
one cannot get him and hold him high,
    and one cannot get him and hold him low.
Thus he is held high by the world.

Commentary on Chapter Fifty-seven

This chapter contrasts two ways of government: nonactive rulership—"taking over the world by not having any tasks"—and active rulership that leads to social unrest and increasing problems. Good government is based on simplicity; it is a simple way of ruling that, in turn, brings about a simple but contented life among the ruled. The people have to be kept in ignorance so that they will be like children or infants (see chapters 49 and 55). They are not to be spoilt but also not to be treated harshly. It is the ruler's duty to keep them in a natural state in which no selfish desires—except, of course, natural desires such as that for food—will occur. The ruler can only keep the people in such a state if he himself is without desire. If he displays desires the people will develop them as well. And if he introduces any kind of rule or regulation, he will violate the natural harmony and simplicity of society. He will create a more and more complex society that becomes increasingly difficult to keep in order. More rules do not make life better, only harder to cope with. "Less is more" when it comes to the Daoist method of rulership.

Fifty-seven

五十七

Order the state with correctness.
Use the military cunningly.
Take over the world by not having any tasks.

How do I know that it is so?

Well,
If there are many taboos and prohibitions in the world,
    the people will become poorer.
If the people have many sharp tools,
    the state and the families will increasingly be in disorder.
If the people have a lot of knowledge and sophistication,
    there will increasingly appear weird things.
If the matters of law are increasingly publicized,
    there will be more robbers and thieves.

Therefore the words of the sage are:
I do not act,
    and the people change by themselves.
I love stillness,
    and the people correct themselves.
I am without task,
    and the people prosper by themselves.
I desire without desire,
    and the people turn to simplicity by themselves.

Commentary on Chapter Fifty-eight

The first stanza of this chapter is connected to the second stanza in chapter 57. The good ruler rules without coming to the fore. He stays hidden and does not introduce orders or restraints. If the government holds on to simplicity, people will naturally lead a simple and contented life. If the ruler turns to action, people will scheme and contend. The *Laozi* certainly does not advocate a civil society. The best rule is not the one in which people strive for political influence and create all sorts of institutions with which to partake in government. Good government, for the *Laozi*, works covertly and "automatically." The people do not feel that they are governed and develop no desire to govern themselves. Good government just allows the natural order to unfold.

The second stanza begins with a saying: good and bad luck are mutually dependent. The *Book of Changes* describes the cosmic course and social life as a rhythm of fortunate and unfortunate events. The course of things changes from one situation to the next and what is today considered good luck, for instance, winning the lottery, can turn out to be bad luck on the next day—when you have an accident with the faster car you bought with the money. Since good and bad luck are just momentary human evaluations that depend one a particular perspective, they are not fixed categories.

Fifty-eight

五十八

Those whose rule is covered up and concealed—
      their people will be pure and sincere.
Those whose rule is open and discriminate—
      their people will be scheming and deceptive.

It is upon bad luck
      that good luck depends.
It is upon good luck
      that bad luck depends.
Who knows where it ends?
There is no correctness as such
      insofar as that which is correct becomes strange again
      and that which is good becomes abnormal again.
The days of the delusion of the people thus continue for long.

Therefore
      be square and do no harm,
      be sharp and do not pierce,
      be straightforward and do not offend,
      be radiant and do not dazzle.

Commentary on Chapter Fifty-nine

A primary strategy for maintaining and preserving both one's body and the state is to be "spare." As a recipe for duration it is both good for attaining long life and for establishing political and social stability. Also, by conserving energy, avoiding friction, and remaining hidden, a situation is created which allows for the "accumulation of efficacy." Towards the end, this chapter mentions once more the "root" (*gen*)—here in the verbal sense of being "rooted." The root is the origin of the energy that allows the plant to live or to have long duration. It is hidden and does not come to the fore. These qualities of the root are shared by the Daoist sage ruler. He is the hidden source of a state's durability.

Fifty-nine

五十九

For ruling humans,
for serving heaven,
    nothing compares to being spare.
Well, by being spare alone,
    early accommodation comes about.
Early accommodation is called:
    multiple accumulation of efficacy [de]—
Multiple accumulation of efficacy
    so that nothing is not overcome.
He by whom nothing is not overcome—
    no one knows his end.
Because no one knows his end,
    he can possess the state.
Because he possesses the mother of the state,
    he can last long.
This is called: being deep-rooted and firmly based.
This is the Dao of long life and lasting vision.

Commentary on Chapter Sixty

The first line of this chapter has been interpreted in many ways. The question is how are small fish fried (or cooked)? Most commentators and translators, however, agree that one fries them very briefly and without much ado. Similarly, the sage ruler should not act much when governing the state. He will not turn things over again and again and come up with complex political recipes. The rule of Dao is, like the preparing of small fish, a simple activity. The simplest form of governing is to let all things occupy their natural positions and fulfill their natural functions. If everything is set up in line with the Dao, the ghosts and spirits won't roam around and cause trouble. It should be recalled that the order of the state and the cosmos also encompasses the realm of the ghosts and spirits—in whose existence people commonly believed in ancient China. Under the rule of an ideal king, the ghosts do not disturb the people and the people do not disturb them. This is at least a reading suggested by the Mawangdui manuscripts. Thus the last stanza would mean that if two, that is, the people and the ghosts, do not harm each other then this will enhance the "efficacy" of the ruler. Even the ghosts will be under his nonactive control.

Sixty

六十

Govern a big state like you fry a small fish!

Set up the world according to the Dao
     and the ghosts will not have spiritual powers.
It is not only that the ghosts will not have spiritual powers,
     it is that their spiritual powers will not harm humans.
It is not only that their spiritual powers will not harm humans,
     it is that the sage will not harm them.

Well,
     two do not harm each other.
Thus efficacy is exchanged and returns to him.

Commentary on Chapter Sixty-one

This chapter talks about political theory and sexuality at the same time. It is important to note that the ancient Chinese terms for "masculine" (*mu*) and "feminine" (*pin*) are not used for humans, but for animals. This chapter is not primarily about men and women, but about the sexual aspect in nature, the division between the sexes that is the condition for reproduction. In sexual interaction, the female "fittingly" takes on the lower position. This position is the one that conceives. Fluids and water flow downwards, so the absorbing position is the one that lies low. At the lowest point, the movement of water comes to rest and so this position is also associated with stillness.

The lower, absorbing position of the female "overcomes" the upper position, the place of the male. Sexual exchange or intercourse is depicted as a competition in which the conceiving element that manages to get fecundated by taking the energies of the other is the "winner." Interestingly enough, sexual competition is connected to the political competition between states. The more powerful position is again the one underneath. Through this position the large state can take possession of the small state—it can make an offer that the small state cannot refuse. The small state can, in turn, submit itself to the greater state, which will not be able to refuse it. The integration of one state into another is initiated by the "lower-lying" state. As in sexuality, the lower-lying "partner" achieves its goal with no resistance from the other partner.

Sixty-one

六十一

A large state is
     low lying waters,
     the female of the world,
     the connection of the world.
The female overcomes the male
     by constant stillness.
Because she is still
     she is therefore fittingly underneath.

By lying lower than a small state
     the great state takes possession of the small state.
By lying lower than a great state
     the small state is taken into possession by the great state.
Thus
     one is low and then takes possession,
     while another is low and then is taken into possession.

Thus
     a great state only wants to unify and nourish people,
     and a small state only wants to unite with and serve
          people.

Well,
     if they all get what they want
     then it suits the great state to lie low.

Commentary on Chapter Sixty-two

The "this" that is spoken of here is the Dao—as Wang Bi and other editors state in their versions of the text. Still, it is not easy to interpret this chapter. The third stanza seems to say that it is better to present the ruler with the teaching of the Dao than with the usual gifts such as disks of jade or horses. Such gifts do not help the ruler as much as good counseling. As is often seen in "classical" Chinese texts, the chapter then points to "antiquity" for an example for the rule of the wise. It is implied that contemporary rulers would do better listening to the advice of the Daoists than indulging in luxury goods. They are admonished to emulate the great examples of the rulers of the past.

The first and particularly the second stanza seem to say that "beautiful words," "good deeds," and even "good men" are not necessarily good. Beautiful words can be used to sell something and polite actions may be just sheer flattery. "Goodness" can be used strategically and turn into its opposite. Given this, the same may be true vice versa. Someone who is not a good speaker and behaves awkwardly may not be the worst kind of person. Read in this way, the first and second stanza would be an implicit criticism of the Confucians and their insistence on proper behavior. What looks good and polite may actually turn out to be superficial or, even worse, deceptive.

Sixty-two

六十二

The Dao
> is the flow of the ten thousand things,
> the treasure of the good person,
> and that by which the person who is not good is
> > protected.

With beautiful words
> one can trade.
With polite deeds
> one can bestow upon others.
That which is not good about people—
> why should it be discarded?

Thus,
> when the Son of Heaven is enthroned
> and the three ministers are put into office
> even if one presents them with disks of jade and then
> > with a team of four horses
> this is not as good as just sitting there and offering "this."
Why was "this" so esteemed in antiquity?
Is it not said:
> "What one strives for one thus gets.
> Those who have done wrong can thereby avoid
> > consequences."
Therefore it is esteemed by the world.

Commentary on Chapter Sixty-three

The first stanza is self-explanatory; it praises the art of nonaction. Being able to rule by nonaction goes along with the ability to tackle developments in their initial stages. If the ruler takes things gravely, and not lightheartedly, he will be aware of the slightest sign of malfunction and can then deal with it without much effort. Ruling a state is similar to keeping one's body healthy—the art of government is an art of prevention. Someone who leads a healthy life will avoid everything that is harmful to the body and will take the appropriate measures when the first symptoms of an illness occur. It is much easier and more effective to prevent illnesses or to tackle them when they have not yet fully developed. Similarly, order in the state is most easily maintained if the arising of disorder is prevented in the first place. Those who have to do only a little—or nothing at all—will be better and more effective rulers than those who invest a lot of activity to deal with a full-blown crisis. Only those who wait too long, the political latecomers, so to speak, will have to act a great deal. They are like doctors who have to treat a patient in the last stages of a sickness. The best doctor—just like the best ruler—has little to do. His or her expertise consists in the ability to take things seriously and, because of this, deal with them with a minimum of effort.

Sixty-three

六十三

Do the nondoing.
Fulfill the task of no task.
Taste the tasteless.

Take the small as great.
Take the little as much.

Respond to anger with efficacy.

Tackle the difficult
    on the basis of what is easy about it.
Realize what is great
    on the basis of what is tiny about it.
That in the world which is difficult
    emerges from what is easy.
That which is great in the world
    emerges from what is tiny.

Therefore the sage will never act greatly.
And thus he can complete what is great.

Well,
One who lightly confirms
    will certainly be of little trustworthiness.
One who often regards things as easy
    will certainly have many difficulties.
Therefore even the sage regards things as difficult.
Therefore he finally has no difficulties.

Commentary on Chapter Sixty-four

The first three stanzas clearly continue the preceding chapter. Again, it is pointed out that prevention and early reaction are the most effective means for coping with dangerous developments and situations. The third stanza consists of three parallel popular sayings that can be understood in line with this maxim, but are commonly seen somewhat differently, namely, as a reminder that even large undertakings begin with little steps. Read in this way they are, rather than a warning to watch out for early symptoms, an encouragement to take on large tasks even if they may seem overwhelming at the beginning. In the context of chapter 64, however, this "popular" interpretation does not seem to be intended. As the fourth stanza once more declares, activism and the taking on of larger projects do not really concur with the Daoist strategy of "nonaction."

The last stanza states that it is not only important to be watchful with respect to "beginnings," but also to end at the proper moment. It is said that the common people often lack this watchfulness and that only the sage is a "master of endings." For any action, timeliness is crucial. It is just as important to complete a task at the right time as it is to take measures early enough to counter bad developments. The most effective way of dealing with things is to avoid and prevent action. If one has to act, however, one has to be cautious enough to stop at the right time. In war, for instance, to euphorically continue to fight after an early success may lead to a fatal defeat later on. All actions have their proper beginning and end. If one misses either of them, one is not in accord with the Dao. This is also true for the course of nature. The seasons have their standard length, and when this is violated the results may be disastrous. When, for instance, the frosts of winter continue into the spring the new crop may be damaged. Timeliness depends as much on right beginnings as on correct endings. In the circular course of time, any ending is also the beginning of something new. If one misses the end, one also misses the next beginning. Right endings and beginnings depend on one another.

146

Sixty-four

六十四

That which is at rest is easily held.
That for which no omen has yet occurred is easily planned for.
That which is tender is easily broken.
That which is fine is easily dispersed.

Act on it when it is not yet present.
Order it when it is not yet in disorder.

A tree that you embrace with both arms emerges from a tiny
    sprout.
A tower that is nine stories high emerges from a basket of
    earth.
Climbing a height of hundreds or thousands of steps begins
    under your feet.

Those who act on things will be defeated by them.
Those who take things in their hands will lose them.
Therefore the sage
        will not act and thus not be defeated,
        will not hold on and thus not lose.

When the people follow their tasks they are continuously
    defeated at the completion.
Therefore it is said:
        Be as careful with respect to the end as with respect to
            the beginning,
        then you will not suffer defeat in your undertakings.

Chapter Sixty-four

Therefore the sage
>desires without desiring
>>and does not esteem goods that are hard to
>>obtain;
>learns without learning
>>and returns to that which the masses of people
>>have passed by.
He is able to support the own course [*ziran*] of the ten
thousand things
>and does not dare to act on them.

Commentary on Chapter Sixty-five

This chapter plays on the double meaning of the word *zhi* which means "to master" in the sense of "to know (how)" and "to rule" (see chapter 33). The ideal ruler does not educate the people. The ruled cannot know—otherwise they would be the "masters" and no longer the "ruled." If people knew, they would lose their quality of being "smiling children," to put it in the words of chapter 49. People only fulfill their tasks naturally and with contentment if they do so more or less unconsciously or "self-so" (*ziran*). This "automaticity," to use a term coined in contemporary psychology, is not only the root of their "great compliance" but also of their freedom from desires and unfulfilled wishes. Here, "dullness" is not something negative. Like "simplicity" it is a quality that signifies that which is in accordance with the Dao. It would be a crime to make the people knowledgeable. This would not only make them unhappy, it would also lead to disorder and contention. The Chinese character translated as "compliance" is *shun* and it consists of the two graphic elements for "river" and "leaf." The Daoist notion of compliance literally means "to go with the flow," just like a leaf that floats on the water. This compliance is therefore not understood negatively as a lack of freedom or self-determination, but rather as an effortless and "easygoing" natural motion.

Sixty-five

六十五

Those who in antiquity practiced the Dao
    did not do this by enlightening the people,
    but by keeping them dull.

Well, when people are difficult to govern
    the reason is that they are knowing.

Thus,
To master the state by making it knowledgeable
    is to commit a crime on the state.
To master the state by making it nonknowledgeable
    is a virtue to the state.

One who constantly masters these two
    also finds the pattern.
To constantly master the found pattern,
    this is called: dark efficacy.
Dark efficacy is profound, far-reaching, and returns with the
  things
    so that the great compliance is reached.

Commentary on Chapter Sixty-six

The chapter begins once again with the praise of that which lies low—a quality associated with water (see chapter 61). It is also a quality that prospective rulers have to adopt. They should designate themselves with the lowest of terms (see chapter 39). The Daoist sage ruler minimizes his personality—he empties himself of all selfishness until nothing "positive" remains. He is devoid of traits and actions, desires and intentions. By putting himself in the lowest position, everybody else, paradoxically, is oriented towards him. Like water he lacks any "personal" form and naturally positions himself at the lowest position; thus he can be the source of (political) life, the nourishing spring in society. Here again, the Daoist rule of reversal applies. The people will cherish and respect most the person who is the least selfish and will yield power to the one who does not pursue it. The sage ruler does not compete with anyone, and so no one competes with him. The ideal Daoist state is one in which only natural forces hold sway. The sage ruler makes use of these natural forces. He does not actively struggle for the support of people or "campaign" against competitors. He adopts a noncontentious strategy that works "self-so." It is because of this lack of active effort that people do not experience the ruler and his government as a burden. He is below the people and thus does not pressure them.

Sixty-six

六十六

Rivers and oceans
> are able to be kings of hundreds of valleys
> because they have the goodness to lie lower than them.

Therefore
> they are able to be kings of hundreds of valleys.

Therefore:
If the sage wishes to be above the people
> he has to place himself below them in words.

If he wishes to be at the front of the people
> he has to put his person behind.

Thus,
> when he is above the people,
> they do not regard him as heavy;
> when he is in front of the people,
> they do not regard him as harmful.

Everybody in the world
> will happily yield to him
> and not become weary of him.

Is this not because he does not contend with anyone?
Thus no one in the world contends with him.

Commentary on Chapter Sixty-seven

The first stanza of this chapter contains a pun. What I have translated as "useless" (*bu xiao* in Chinese) means more literally "not resembling anything."[11] However, the expression is also used as a self-depreciating or modest and polite term for designating oneself when addressing elders or superiors. By using it one claims either to be less worthy than others or to have no specific virtues, talents, or traits that could fulfill a purpose. In this way, one designates oneself as "useless"—and thus, following the Daoist paradoxical logic, claims to be the only person suitable for becoming a ruler. The "me" in the first line is once more the sage ruler who declares himself as useless and thus the one predestined for taking on the only position of nonaction in the state, that is, the position of the head of government. The useless is at the same time the greatest—and thus he does not resemble anyone else in the state. All others have their specific functions; only the ruler has none.

The second part of the chapter is also based on paradoxes. The three "treasures" of compassion, frugality, and "placing oneself behind" turn into their opposites: defensive compassion turns into offensive courage, frugality leads to spending, and the one who stays in the back will become the leader. These results can only be attained if they are rooted in their opposite qualities, otherwise they will lead to failure. The first of the three treasures is the topic of the last stanzas. Hanfeizi's commentary on this chapter interprets compassion as the virtue of motherhood. A mother cares compassionately for her children and so she will instinctively defend them when they are in danger. Thus her defensive compassion can turn into an offensive, belligerent force. If one's courage is paradoxically rooted in compassion, one

---

11. The term *xiao*, particularly in the form that appears in the Mawangdui manuscripts, can also mean "little." If it were translated in this way the first stanza would just be tautological: "Everybody in the world calls me great, great and not small," etc.

will be able to triumph in battle. If a state has a ruler who has motherly compassion, it will be successful in war and is well protected or "encircled."

Sixty-seven

六十七

Everybody in the world calls me great,
    great and useless.
Well,
    that which is useless alone
    can therefore be great.
If it were useful, how long would it be minute?

Well,
    I continuously have three treasures
    that I hold and treasure.
The first is: compassion.
The second is: frugality.
The third is: not daring to be in front of the world.
Well,
    compassion so that one can be courageous,
    frugality so that one can be generous,
    not daring to be in front of the world so that one can be
        the head of those who constitute the tools.
Now,
    if one abandons compassion and is courageous,
    if one abandons frugality and is generous,
    if one abandons staying back and goes to the front,
one will die.
Well, with compassion
    in battle one will win,
    in guarding one will be firm.

If heaven is about to establish something
it will seemingly encircle it with compassion.

Commentary on Chapter Sixty-eight

The strategies that match "heaven" or "nature" (*tian*), and are thus in accord with the Dao will lead to success in politics as well as in battle. The first stanza describes this Daoist tactic. One does not seek open or direct confrontation, but practices a strategy of retreat and of taking oneself back. In line with the virtue of "compassion" described in the preceding chapter, the Daoist warrior does not rely on the offensive; rather, his attitude towards war is rooted in defense.

The Daoist "art of war" is connected to the art of using or employing people. This chapter expresses once more the Daoist idea that the leader will, paradoxically, place himself below the ruled, and then "naturally" be nominated as their leader (see, for instance, the previous chapter). This is, as the last line states, the "golden" way of antiquity, the time when things were still in order. Daoists, like the Confucians, support their argumentation by referring to ancient times as a model for the present.

Sixty-eight

六十八

Thus,
Those who are good warriors
    are not belligerent.
Those who are good at battling
    do not get angry.
Those who defeat their enemies
    do not engage them.
Those who are good at employing others
    place themselves below them.

This is called: the efficacy of not contending.
This is called: employing others.
This is called: matching heaven.
It is the ultimate of antiquity.

Commentary on Chapter Sixty-nine

The saying in the first stanza confirms the tactical guidelines that have been mentioned in the two preceding chapters. A winning strategy rests on defense and evasion. The enemy will then take the initiative and, so to speak, "shoot himself in the foot." Defensive tactics are a practical application of the maxim of "nonacting and nothing is undone" and of the logic of the paradox. One acts most effectively if one manages to let others do the action.

In order to be successful, one has to be watchful. The third stanza can be read in connection with chapter 64's advice to be mindful of beginnings. Without enemies one tends to become negligent and so is probably bound for disaster. In politics, bodily health, and warfare it is of the utmost importance to be watchful or "worrisome." It is this "motherly" characteristic that is in accord with the Dao (the "mother," see chapters 1, 20, 25, 52, and 59) and, because of this, eventually results in success.

Sixty-nine

六十九

With respect to the usage of weapons there is a saying:
"I do not dare to be the lord,
    and rather be the host.
I do not dare to go an inch forward,
    and rather retreat a foot."

This means:
    taking steps without taking steps;
    rolling up the sleeves without baring the arms;
    taking hold without the force of weapons;
    defying without engaging the enemy.

Of the disasters none is greater than
    not having an enemy.
Without an enemy,
    I come close to losing my treasures.

Thus,
    When weapons are taken up
    and the opposing sides are of comparable power,
    then the worrisome will win.

Commentary on Chapter Seventy

This chapter once more plays with the double meaning of the verb "to know (how)" or "to master" (*zhi*, see for instance chapters 33 and 56). The words of the sage are easily mastered and practiced—there is nothing one needs to do or learn. The paradoxical mastery of the Daoist art (of rulership) only demands that one minimizes one's actions, deeds, and intentions. Still, the sage is the only human who perfectly masters this art of dehumanization. The empty hub at the center of the wheel is singular. Even though it is, "theoretically," easy to follow the path of emptiness and nonaction, there can only be one person in this central position. Echoing the first stanza, the third stanza corresponds perfectly to this Daoist logic of rulership. The sage ruler becomes the ruler because he is the only one who does not take on any specific task—he masters nothing. By mastering nothing, the sage ruler becomes the master of all because no one can master him. This is how the sage ruler's esteem is constituted. The chapter then concludes by praising the sage's frugality and simplicity—he wears coarse clothing—which, paradoxically, expresses his exceptional worth.

Sometimes this chapter is read as a melancholic "complaint" from the presumable author of the text that people do not understand the Daoist message and are thus unable to put it into practice. I do not believe in a personal authorship or a personal narrator within the *Laozi*. I rather think that the "I" that appears in the text—and particularly in this chapter—is the "I" of the prospective reader or listener, namely the one who aspires to become a sage ruler. According to my interpretation, this chapter does not voice an author's concern about being misunderstood, but rather expresses the Daoist rule of paradox: Only a single sage ruler is able to master the "easy" art of nonmastery—and this is perfectly fine. The chapter does not decry a lack of intelligent readership, but points out that ideally only one person will master the teaching of the Dao—and therefore will not be mastered by anyone else. The chapter points out that the *Laozi* is ideally intended for only one reader or listener.

Seventy

七十

My words
    are easily mastered
    and easily practiced,
but there is no one in the world who can master them
and no one who can practice them.

Well,
words have an ancestor,
tasks have a lord.

Well,
    only since I master nothing
    no one masters me.

Those who master are few.
Therefore I am esteemed.
Therefore
    a sage wears coarse clothes
    but contains jade.

Commentary on Chapter Seventy-one

This chapter continues the discussion about the mastery (the know-how) of nonmastery. The highest form of mastery is paradoxical. The know-how of the sage consists in having no know-how, in not taking on any particular function in the state. The most effective of all arts is this negative art. If a ruler does not master this art, then this is a blemish. Only those who know about this blemish, those who see this paradoxical blemish as a blemish, will succeed in the art of mastery or good government.

The Daoist art of nonmastery and non-know-how is distinctively different from the Socratic version of wisdom by nonknowledge. Socratic nonknowledge portrays the philosopher as a searcher for wisdom who has an insight into the insufficiency of sense-knowledge and traditional truths. The true seeker of wisdom begins a quest for higher knowledge that can be fully understood as true—and this is hard to obtain. Daoist nonmastery pertains only to having no specific know-how. It is based on the paradoxical maxim of "doing nothing and nothing is undone" and is basically a political strategy.

Seventy-one

七十一

To master not-mastering—
     this is the highest.
To not master not-mastering—
     this is a blemish.

Therefore
     the sage is without blemish
     because he identifies the blemish as blemish.
Therefore he is without blemish.

Commentary on Chapter Seventy-two

When the people do not respect their leaders and are not afraid of violating the law, the state is in peril. If, conversely, the people respect those in power, particularly, of course, the sage ruler, then there will be order and political stability. On the other hand, the ruler is not simply to be feared. Chapter 17 states that the one who is feared is only the third best ruler (although still not the worst). The ruler has to, in turn, make life easy for his subjects and provide for their needs. As chapter 17 put it: "Of the best of all rulers people will only know that he exists." The ruler is obliged not to harm the people and not to be a weight on their shoulders. His rule is not to be based on selfish interests in power and wealth, but on the intention to be in harmony with the Dao. If he does not suppress his people, the people will not become weary of him (compare with chapter 66). Thus, a reciprocal cycle is established. The people respect the ruler and fear the law while the ruler serves the well-being of the people. In this way they support one another and there is no contention or dispute.

Seventy-two

If the people do not fear the fearful
    then that which is greatly fearful is about to come.

Do not limit them in their dwellings.
Do not oppress them in their livelihood.
Well,
    only if they are not oppressed,
    will they not become weary.

Therefore the sage
    will master himself and not make himself seen,
    will care for himself and not hold himself in esteem.
Thus he rejects the one and takes the other.

Commentary on Chapter Seventy-three

To be "daring" is at odds with the Daoist preference for restraint. A sage does not dare to act (chapters 3 and 64), to be in the front (chapter 67), or to be the lord (chapter 69). Such daring exposes oneself to dangers and possible defeat. Instead of an offensive mode of action, the Daoist sage dares, paradoxically, not to dare. Not to act or take the initiative can also be understood as a way of being daring.

The defensive nature of Daoism is also the topic of the second stanza. Without confrontation the sage overcomes his opponents. The nonaction of the sage goes along with his silence. By not giving any orders the people naturally follow him. The importance of planning ahead that the text speaks of corresponds to the importance of being aware of "beginnings" that is discussed in chapters 63 and 64.

Seventy-three

七十三

To be courageous in daring
    results in death.
To be courageous in not-daring
    results in life.
Of the two,
    one benefits and the other harms.
Who knows the reasons for the bad things brought about by
    heaven?

The Dao of heaven—
    Without contending, it is good at winning.
    Without speaking, it is well responded to.
    Without calling, it is approached spontaneously.
    Being at ease, it is good at planning ahead.

The net of heaven is greatly extended.
Its mesh is wide, but it misses nothing.

As opposed to the standard version of the text, the Mawangdui manuscripts have the term for "death penalty" in the first sentence (the Wang Bi version, as well as other early editions, simply has the word "death") and thus explicitly address this issue. The existence of the death penalty results, in typically paradoxical fashion, in a situation in which it will not be used. The chapter describes a Daoist model of deterrence. If the people enjoy living their life, they will fear death. If they fear death, they will be afraid of the death penalty. Under these circumstances nobody will "dare" (compare with the preceding chapter for the Daoist view on "daring") to break the law and interfere in the natural order of society.

It is quite obvious that the "I" that occurs in the second sentence is, again, that of the sage ruler. Only the sage ruler is able to watch over the death penalty. He alone, because of his empty self, will not use it for his own benefit or to get rid of any opponents. Only the completely impartial ruler who acts in accord with the Dao can be entrusted with the power over life and death. If anyone replaced him in this function, there would be disaster. In this model, the death penalty only works in a preventative manner. It works as long as it is not used. It makes itself obsolete. If a leader with personal interests makes active use of the death penalty he will create antagonisms and opposition. The people will look at his rule as a tyranny and plot against him. In the end those who actively use the death penalty will ultimately become its victims—one may think of Robespierre and many other examples. If one establishes a social climate of violence and revenge, one can hardly exempt oneself from that climate. When the powers shift, one is likely to be treated as one treated others.

Seventy-four

七十四

If the people are not at all afraid of death,
     how should they be frightened by the death penalty?
If people are at all afraid of death,
     and if I will capture and execute those who act wrongly,
     who then will dare to do so?
If the people are to fear death at all,
     then there must always be a hangman.

Well,
     intending to replace the hangman in hanging,
     this is to replace the wood cutter in cutting wood.
When the wood cutter is replaced,
     the hand is seldom unharmed.

Commentary on Chapter Seventy-five

In life it is important not to live excessively; only thus can decay and an early death be avoided. All kinds of gluttony harm life. In the state, the famine that people suffer from is caused by the excesses of their rulers. A bad regent can literally tax people to death. Such a shortsighted ruler who only aims at quick personal gain and takes on "activist" measures undermines his authority and causes disorder in the state—this is what the first and second stanza imply.

Similarly, living excessively treats death lightly—and living so, one is bound to die early. Just as an excessive ruler ruins his state through his striving for a "good life," so a person can ruin his or her body by indulging in all kinds of excesses. To live in accord with the Dao, on the contrary, means to not engage in an active pursuit of what one may desire. To live one's life actively means at the same time, as stated in chapter 50, to approach death. The "thirteen companions of life" are also the "thirteen companions of death." Only those who protect their life and do not waste or squander their resources can be labeled "wise."

Seventy-five

七十五

As to the hunger of people—
>because the taxes taken on food are too high,
>therefore there is hunger.

As to the disorder among people—
>because those above engage in action,
>therefore the people are in disorder.

As to the people looking lightly at death—
>because they strive so intensely in life,
>therefore they look at death lightly.

Well,
>alone not to act for the sake of one's living,
>this is wiser than to esteem life.

Commentary on Chapter Seventy-six

The soft and hard are, respectively, the qualities of being alive and being dead. That which lives is pliant and flexible, whereas that which dies loses these qualities and becomes hard and brittle. In nature these qualities signal the state of an animal, a plant, or a human being. In the context of the *Laozi*, this "rule" can also be applied to the state of a society and to strategies of government and warfare. Those who want to lead a state or an army have to follow the tactics of the supple and flexible if they want to survive. Those who rule rigidly or seek confrontation in warfare will be "broken" and suffer defeat. The soft and the weak are superior to the hard and the strong and will eventually overcome it—as chapters 36 and 78 explain.

The last stanza identifies the soft and the weak as that which is above, and the hard and rigid as that which is below. This is in contrast to other chapters (like chapter 61) which identify the lower position as the dominating one. Here the terms "below" and "above" may therefore be read in the sense of "inferior" and "superior" (as, for instance, in Henricks's translation).[12]

The soft and the weak and, by analogy, that which is alive are, in this chapter, clearly seen as more desirable than the hard, rigid, and the dead. This general tendency in the *Laozi* is, interestingly enough, not the dominant position in the *Zhuangzi*. In contrast, the *Zhuangzi* affirms the equal validity of life and death and thus of the soft and the hard. It not only praises the soft as the quality of the living, but, equally, the hard as the quality of the dead, and it states quite famously: "Your body should be like the branch of a dried up tree, your heart should be like dead ashes."[13] This equanimity towards life and death is typical for the *Zhuangzi* and may

---

12. Robert G. Henricks, *Lao-Tzu: Te-Tao Ching; A New Translation Based on the Recently Discovered Ma-Wang-Tui Texts* (New York: Ballantine, 1989).

13. *Zhuangzi yinde* (Beijing: 1946), 63/23/42.

be interpreted as a philosophical "refinement" in comparison with the *Laozi*.[14]

14. See the chapters on "The Body (Of Infants and Corpses)" and "Life and Death" in my *Daoism Explained: From the Dream of the Butterfly to the Fishnet Allegory* (Chicago: Open Court, 2004).

Seventy-six

七十六

When alive
    men are supple and soft.
When dead
    they are, stretched out and reaching the end, hard
      and rigid.
When alive
    the ten thousand things and the grasses and trees
    are supple and pliant.
When dead
    they are dried out and brittle.

Therefore it is said:
The hard and the rigid
    are the companions of death.
The supple and the soft, the delicate and the fine
    are the companions of life.

If a weapon is rigid,
    it will not win.
If a tree is rigid,
    it is reaching the end.

The rigid and great
    settle below.
The supple and the soft, the delicate and the fine
    settle above.

Commentary on Chapter Seventy-seven

As stated in chapter 40, reversal is the movement of the Dao. The first stanza describes such reversals in nature. "Heaven" or nature tends to even things out. Unfortunately, the chapter implies, humans often do not follow the rule of reversal: The rich get richer and the poor get poorer. This leads to "unnatural" circumstances in society. It is the sage ruler's duty to prevent such tendencies and instead develop and keep society in accord with nature and the Dao. If the sage is successful in bringing society in line with the natural rhythm of giving and taking, then there will be no shortages of supplies, no lack of food, and people will contribute to the enrichment of nature through their agricultural activities. Only a society that operates in accord with the Dao will be able to prosper in this way. In such a society, the sage ruler will claim nothing for himself and even refuse to be honored. His rule is not based on human reverence but on being in harmony with the Dao.

Seventy-seven

七十七

The Dao of heaven is like flexing a bow:
     what is high is lowered,
     what is below is lifted,
     where there is abundance, it is taken away,
     where there is a lack, it is added to.

Thus
the Dao of heaven
     takes away where there is abundance and gives where
          there is a lack;
the Dao of humans
     takes away where there is a lack and offers more where
          there is abundance.

Well,
     who can, when having an abundance, still offer more to
          heaven?
Only the one who has the Dao.

Therefore
     the sage makes but does not possess,
     does not reside where he completes his undertaking.
Thus is his unwillingness to be looked upon as worthy.

Commentary on Chapter Seventy-eight

Water is an image of the Dao and a guide for the sage. All things gravitate to the low-lying body of water (compare chapter 61). In chapter 78, however, other characteristics of water are more important. While water is the softest of all materials, it still can tackle and overcome the hardest stone. It cannot be "changed." It permanently and naturally follows its steady course without any effort. It practices the art of "nonaction and nothing is undone" (*wu wei er wu bu wei*) that the sage ruler takes as his model. Like water, the ruler takes on the lowest position—he claims nothing for himself and takes on only depreciative self-designations but, because of this, he is, without contention, unanimously accepted as the leader. Therefore "right words are like the reverse" as this chapter concludes—and this is the most concise expression of the rule of the paradox in the *Laozi*.

This chapter, particularly its first stanza, can also be interpreted sexually.[15] Softness and smoothness are qualities traditionally associated with the female whereas the hard and the stiff are associated with the male. In sexuality—and not only in human sexuality—these two components come together. Sexual intercourse is thus described as a competition between the sexes in which the female overcomes the male. She manages to become fecundated and thus to be the source of reproduction. This is "known" by everyone—but normally men hold on to their "tactics" of the stiff and the hard. Only the sage ruler is able to "know the masculine and maintain the feminine" as chapter 28 states. In this way the sage ruler's functioning in the state can be associated not only with water, but also with the female. By taking on female qualities he nourishes society like a mother (see chapters 1, 20, 25, 52, and 59).

---

15. See the chapter on sexuality in my *The Philosophy of the Daodejing* (New York: Columbia University Press, 2006).

Seventy-eight

七十八

Nothing in the world
        is smoother and softer than water;
but nothing surpasses it in
        tackling the stiff and the hard,
because it is not to be changed.

That water defeats the solid,
that the soft defeats the hard:
        No one in the world who does not know this,
        but still no one is able to practice it.

Therefore the words of the sage are:
To take on the shameful in the state,
        this is to be lord of the altars of earth and grain.
To take on the unfavorable in the state,
        this is to be king of the world.

Right words are like the reverse.

Commentary on Chapter Seventy-nine

This chapter can be explained along the following lines: The duties of a ruler include, along with politics and warfare, the supervision of legal matters and taxation. The main objective, from a Daoist point of view, is to prevent the arising of disputes in the first place—just as the best attitude towards war is to avoid it. Even if a grumble or a grievance is settled, a somewhat poisoned atmosphere will probably still remain. Such quarrels are not conducive to a frictionless society.

Contractual tallies in ancient China consisted of two parts. The right half remained with the side that had some claims, whereas the left one remained with the indebted one. The ruler would thus normally be identified with the right side of a tally because everyone was indebted to him.[16] The Daoist rule of the paradox, however, implies that the ruler who can rightly claim everything will, in effect, claim nothing of his subjects. The ruler holds on to the right half but does not use it—particularly, not to the disadvantage of the ruled. His rule is empowered only by his "efficacy" (*de*). In this way, he remains unchallenged and also prevents grievances. At the same time, he does not overtax the people so that even if he had all the right sides, he would not use them to his personal advantage. Similarly, the ruler does not grant any special favors; he does not treat a particular group as his kinsmen. Only by upholding his total impartiality can he prevent both grumbles among the people and resentment against him and his powers.

---

16. It should be noted that most versions, including the Wang Bi edition and Mawangdui B, have the sage hold on to the *left* side of the tally. I, however, follow Robert G. Henricks's decision to read the chapter as it appears in Mawangdui A. See Henricks, *Lao-Tzu*.

Seventy-nine

七十九

When a great grumble is settled
    there will necessarily remain some grumble.
How then can something good be done?

Therefore the sage
    holds on to the right portions of the tally
    but does not burden people with it.

Thus,
One who possesses efficacy
    takes care of the tallies;
One who does not possess efficacy
    takes care of the taxes.

Well,
    the Dao of heaven does not establish any kinships,
    it is always with the good person.

Commentary on Chapter Eighty

This chapter offers a description of the ideal Daoist state. A society of moderation lives in peace with the world. All things are present, but many of them are never used. The military and the death penalty (people "take death seriously," see chapter 74) fulfill their deterring functions and are thus never called to action. Along with the lack of any desire for the external or internal use of force goes a lack of desire for luxury goods or for leaving one's country. Everyone remains in one's place and no cravings arise (see chapter 46). All functions are thus fulfilled. In such a state there is contentment. In line with the rule of reversal, restraint turns into satisfaction. Food, clothing, and the necessary goods are provided for, and so all lead happy and peaceful lives.

Since the state returns to the most ancient and simple form of script, it also returns to the simplest form of administration and government. This is an implicit criticism of the Confucian political ideal that refers to a legend found in the *Book of Changes* (*Yijing*). The Confucians assumed that society was established by ancient sage rulers who invented the basic elements of a "civilized" society. Among these was the Chinese script: "In early antiquity knots were tied for the purpose of government. The sages of later generations exchanged these with scriptural records in order to rule over the many officials and to oversee the masses of the people."[17] Read in conjunction with this passage, chapter 80 of the *Laozi* obviously advocates a return to a "pre-Confucian" type of government.

---

17. *Xici xia*. Translated on the basis of: Gao Heng, ed., *Zhou Yi Dazhuan jin zhu* (Jinan: Ji Lu shushe, 1979), 567.

Primitism

Eighty

八十

A small state, few people.

Let there be a militia and weapons,
    but people do not use them.
Let people take death seriously,
    and migrating is far from their mind.
There are boats and carriages
    which no one rides.
There are shields and swords
    which no one takes up.
Let people return to the use of knotted cords for writing.

Sweet be the food.
Beautiful be the clothing.
Happy be the customs.
Peaceful be the homes.

Neighboring states are within the distance of sight,
    and the sounds of chickens and dogs are mutually heard.
But people reach old age and die
    without traveling back and forth.

Commentary on Chapter Eighty-one

The one who is trusted and good is the sage ruler. In his words he is modest and full of restraint; he does not talk "beautifully." In fact, he is mostly silent (see chapter 23). By designating himself with depreciative and nonbeautiful titles he becomes trustworthy (see chapter 66). The one that lacks specific knowledge or abilities, that is, the one who *masters* the Dao of rulership, is "erudite." By not knowing anything he is the master of all. Only the ruled have specific knowledge and abilities that allow them to master a specific function. Their knowledge is different from that of the sage (see chapter 33). The Daoist ruler is also single—there is not more than one ruler at a time. What is good is not manifold. Only the single ruler can unite the people—he provides for the oneness of society (see chapter 39). As the empty center of society, the sage ruler does not accumulate any personal possessions. His sole function is to be the pivot of society, and thus he affects everything in society not for his own sake but for the sake of all others (see chapter 77). By providing for all others, no one has a reason to contend with him. He does not contend, and so no one contends with him (see chapters 66, 68, and 73).

Eighty-one

八十一

Trustworthy words are not beautiful.
Beautiful words are not trustworthy.

The one who knows is not erudite.
The one who is erudite does not know.

What is good is not a lot.
What is a lot is not good.

The sage does not accumulate.
> By thus providing for others he gains for himself.
> By thus giving to others he has more for himself.

Thus,
The Dao of heaven
> benefits without doing harm.
The Dao of humans
> has effects without contending.

Appendix

Different Versions of the *Daodejing*: A Comparison with Special Consideration of Chapter 19.[1]

I.

In 1993, a major excavation was made near the Chinese village of Guo-dian 郭店 close to the city of Jingmen 荆門 in the province of Hubei 湖北. Here, not far from where the capital city of the state of Chu 楚, Jingmencheng, was located in the times of the "Warring States," a tomb of a member of the political elite of Chu had been discovered. On the basis of the characteristics of the tomb and the objects it contained, the site could be dated back to the time between the middle of the fourth and the beginning of the third century BCE.[2]

Despite the tomb's having been subjected to robberies two times before its archaeological investigation, Chinese scientists were able to bring a number of objects to light of day. Among the discovered texts were several bamboo strips with fragments of the *Laozi* 老子. Thus there was now, after the excavations in Mawangdui 馬王堆 in the early 1970s, a second ancient manuscript of the *Laozi*—and the bamboo texts from Guodian are, seemingly, at least a century older than the silk manuscripts from Mawangdui, which stem back to early Han 漢 times.[3]

---

1. A German version of this appendix was published in 1999: "Verschiedene Versionen des *Laozi*. Ein Vergleich mit besonderer Berücksichtigung des 19. Kapitels," *Monumenta Serica* 47: 285–302. I translate the original version of this article without commenting on scholarship in English that has since been published, most notably Robert G. Henricks, *Lao Tzu's Tao Te Ching: A Translation of the Startling New Documents Found at Guodian* (New York: Columbia University Press, 2000).

2. See the report on the excavation published by the Museum of the City of Jingmen in the province of Hubei 湖北省荆門市博物館, "Jingmen Guodian yi hao Chu mu" 荆門郭店一號楚墓 (Chu tomb no. 1 in Guodian, Jingmen), *Wenwu* 文物 7 (1997): 35–48.

3. On dating the Mawangdui silk manuscripts, see Michael Friedrich, "Zur Datie-rung zweier Handschriften des *Daode jing*," *Text-Kritische Beiträge* 2 (1996): 105–17.

The bamboo texts of the *Laozi* consist of three sets (in the following: texts A, B, and C) of largely intact bamboo strips of slightly varying size, each of which is inscribed with one column of characters. Text A consists of 39 strips 39.2 centimeters in length and corresponds—if the common division of chapters of the *textus receptus* (the Wang Bi 王 弼 version[4]) is applied—to the present chapters 19, 66, 46 (beginning and end), 30 (beginning and middle), 15, 64 (end), 37, 63, 2, 32, 25, 5 (middle), 16 (beginning), 64 (beginning) 56, 57, 55, 44, 40, and 9. Text B consists altogether of 18 strips, each of which is 30.6 centimeters in length, and corresponds to the present-day chapters 59, 48 (beginning), 20 (beginning), 13, 41, 52 (middle), 45, and 54. Text C consists of 14 strips, each of which is 26.5 centimeters in length, and corresponds to the present-day chapters 17, 18, 35, 31 (middle and end), and 64 (end). Thus, the bamboo texts comprise about two-fifths of the later *Daodejing* 道德經. Thirty-one of the eighty-one chapters of the *textus receptus* are, at least in part, already found in the bamboo texts.[5] The characters used "obviously have the specific characteristics of the type of writing used in the state of Chu during the period of the Warring States."[6] With respect to "the type of writing used in the state of Chu," however, the greatly varying versions of the final passage of present-day chapter 64 in texts A and C—particularly in regard to the writing of individual characters—demonstrate that there was no standardized script. Rather, there was a degree of arbitrariness in writing individual characters.

Like the silk manuscripts from Mawangdui, the bamboo texts are not yet clearly divided into the later chapters, although there are some rudimentary forms of punctuation—altogether nine black markers in text A and three such markers in text B, out of which all except two (one each in texts A and B) are found in between today's chapters. Still, the order of the individual passages seems to indicate

---

4. On the Wang Bi edition of the *Laozi*, see Rudolf G. Wagner, "The Wang Bi Recension of the *Laozi*," *Early China* 14 (1989): 27–54. Cf. also the collation of various editions including the Wang Bi version in Shima Kunio 島邦男, *Rōshi kōsei* 老 子校正 (Tokyo: Kyūko shoin, 1973) as well as William G. Boltz, "The *Lao tzu* text that Wang Bi and Ho-shang Kung never saw," *Bulletin of the School of Oriental and African Studies* 48.3 (1985): 493–501.

5. Cf. *Guodian Chu mu zhujian* 郭店一號楚墓 (The bamboo documents in the Chu tomb at Guodian) (Shijiazhuang: Wenwu, 1998), 111.

6. Museum of the City of Jingmen, "Jingmen Guodian yi hao Chu mu," 47.

that the division into chapters which later became prevalent already significantly influenced the composition of the text at this early stage. Although the textual parts of the later *Daodejing* appear in the bamboo texts in an order completely different from both the Mawangdui texts and the *textus receptus* (where, as it is known, the sections *dao* 道 and *de* 德 are in the reverse order of the Mawangdui texts), the sentences and verses that became clustered together as chapters in the historically younger versions (if they are present at all) still appear in their present-day conjunction. With only one exception (the later chapter 64 is formed out of parts that are separated in text A and one of which appears a second time in a different version in text C) the materials that later became chapters are already grouped together in the bamboo texts. The later versions only vary, exchange, or extend these clusters. The order of the bamboo texts thus demonstrates that the later chapter divisions were essentially made where they had "traditionally" been, even when the general sequence was subject to change. Metaphorically speaking, the pieces of the jigsaw puzzle were put together in different ways and there were quite a few pieces added over time, but the individual contours of the pieces, once they were drawn, remained largely the same. Whereas the general picture was fundamentally renewed, the structure of the individual elements, as documented in the bamboo texts, remained remarkably unaltered.

While the chapter sequence of the bamboo texts is reminiscent neither of the Mawangdui texts nor of the *textus receptus*—and also not of the order of passages as they appear in the commentaries on the *Laozi* within the *Hanfeizi* 韓非子 —a closer look at the structure still reveals an interesting feature: Both in the Mawangdui manuscripts and in the *textus receptus*, the chapters present in the bamboo texts are often found in close proximity to each other. Of the eight chapters 13–20 in the *textus receptus* seven are, either as a whole or in part, included in the bamboo texts (chapter 14 is not present, although the chapters are separated at the point where chapter 14 would appear). Similarly, five (all except chapter 53) out of the six chapters 52–57 are at least fragmentarily found in the bamboo texts. The six chapters 30–32 and 44–46 as well as the four chapters 40–41 and 63–64 are all, at least in fragments, included in the bamboo texts. This means that 22 out of the 31 *Laozi* chapters (more than two thirds) present in the bamboo texts were grouped together in the *textus receptus*, but there they appear in a different order and in a new sequence. Accordingly, it seems, quite surprisingly, that later editions of the *Laozi* conceived of materials as related which, for the most part, were not yet seen as belonging together in the bamboo texts. This might suggest that later editors—either aware of or unaware of the version of the bamboo manuscripts—found that those materials were either with respect to their style or content homogenous and grouped them together in new chapter sequences.

With respect to their contents, the bamboo texts focus on the art of government through personal or bodily cultivation. This cultivation is supposed to bring about a stable, safe, and well-functioning organism that is to serve as a model for the political body. In the sequences of chapters 13–20 and 52–57 this issue is of prime importance.[7] Out of the nine chapters in the *textus receptus* (7, 9, 13, 16, 26, 44, 52, 54, and 66) that contain the character *shen* 身 for "body,"—and in the *Laozi* this often means the body of the ruler and is a way of referring to himself, a way of saying "I"—as many as seven (all except 7 and 26) are found in the bamboo texts and all of these contain the character *shen* (with the exception of chapter 16, but the respective parallel verse in chapter 52 is present). While the character *shen* appears only in one-ninth of the chapters in the *textus receptus*, it appears in a fifth of all chapters in the bamboo texts—and thus, if the relative frequency is taken in account, it appears nearly twice as often. Moreover, in the bamboo texts one particularly finds those chapters, such as 15 and 55, that discuss the ruler's body. The bodily cultivation of the ruler—which should not be identified with the bodily exercises of later Daoist practice that aimed at, for instance, the attainment of immortality—as a precondition for an optimized government of the state and the world is thus *a*, if not *the*, core issue in the bamboo texts (and, specifically, in texts A and B).

A second philosophical focus of the bamboo texts is the Daoist (political) art of "nonaction" (*wu wei* 無為), or "action without action." Since the Mawangdui manuscripts lack these respective phrases, it had been speculated that this famous maxim only represents a later textual development, but the bamboo texts impressively prove that the art of government through nonaction certainly has ancient roots.

---

7. Cf. my comments on chapters 13 and 55 in the version of the Mawangdui manuscripts (there, these are chapters 57 and 18) in Hans-Georg Moeller, trans., *Laotse: Tao Te King; Die Seidentexte von Mawangdui* (Frankfurt/Main: Fischer, 1995), 79 and 175–76.

The strategy of *wu wei* is addressed several times in the bamboo texts, sometimes explicitly and sometimes implicitly, for instance in (present-day) chapters 2, 37, 48, 57, 63, and 64. This topic thus also appears in the bamboo texts with a higher frequency than in the Mawangdui manuscripts and the *textus receptus*. It is particularly worth mentioning that the formula "nonaction and nothing is not done" (*wu wei er wu bu wei* 無為而無不為) from chapter 48, which is lacking in the Mawangdui manuscripts, is, in an early variation, present in the bamboo texts.

If one looks at these two core issues in the bamboo texts (bodily cultivation of the ruler, and the maxim of nonaction) in conjunction, then it becomes obvious that the bamboo texts represent a form of "political" Daoism, that is, a Daoism for rulers. They are obviously primarily addressed to the regent(s), and they propagate—in line with later versions—an ideal of personal and behavioral education of the ruler and, thereby, of the social whole.

Of course, the bamboo texts cannot provide definite answers to the questions about the authorship of the *Laozi* and the exact stages of its history. The only thing that they factually prove is that certain parts of the *Daodejing* existed in early written forms at the beginning of the third century BCE. But the bamboo strips contain no hint of the identity of an author or the date of the text's composition. These texts can only give rise to new speculations about these issues and can be used to critically review the extant theories.

The Chinese scholar Guo Yi 郭沂 has presented a new theory of the origin of the *Daodejing* based on the discovery of the bamboo texts.[8] Guo believes that the Guodian bamboo texts represent an original and complete text, a sort of urtext of the *Laozi*. He also argues that they are linguistically and philosophically clearer than later versions (such as the Mawangdui texts and the *textus receptus*). His argumentation culminates in the claim that the authorship of these texts should be ascribed to the historical Laozi. This person, according to Guo, is the Lao Dan 老聃, who is known through the Laozi biography in the *Shiji* 史記. Supposedly, he was a contemporary of Confucius, had once philosophically instructed the latter, and was employed as a court archivist. The present-day *Laozi*, as it is known in the variations of the

---

8. Guo Yi, "*Cong Guodian Chu jian 'Laozi' kan Laozi qi ren qi shu*," 從郭店楚簡 "老子" 看老子其人其書 (Laozi, the man and the text, seen from the perspective of Guodian bamboo texts), *Zhexue yanjiu* 哲學研究 7 (1998): 47–55.

Mawangdui manuscripts and the *textus receptus*, Guo believes, goes back to another person who is also mentioned in the *Shiji* biography, namely, the Grand Historian Dan (*Taishi Dan* 太史聃), who was active in the state of Qin 秦 and lived more than a hundred years after Confucius. On the basis of the *Shiji*, Guo calculates that it was this *Taishi Dan* who, between 384 and 374 BCE, crossed the mountain pass to the West and, on this occasion, dictated the text in two sections and 5000 words to a border guard. The Great Historian, Guo concludes, had incorporated the earlier materials written by the court archivist Lao Dan and added attacks against Confucianism in order to make the text more in line with the Legalist state doctrine of the state of Qin, which finally united China militarily and politically. Thus it was, according to Guo, this new and enlarged *Laozi* that was studied by and commented on, for instance, by the Legalist philosopher Hanfeizi in the third century BCE.

This somewhat adventurous theory is, on the one hand, based on a nearly literary trust in the words of the *Shiji*, and it explains away the obvious self-contradictions and obscurities of the *Shiji* with the help of supposedly logical conclusions drawn from comparisons with other sources. On the other hand, it is based on the rather deeply rooted and more or less "traditional" belief in the personal authorship of the *Laozi* in particular and ancient Chinese philosophical texts in general. If one neither trusts the *Shiji* as much as Guo Yi nor holds on to the paradigm of personal authorship—and is instead more influenced by the postmodern paradigm of the suspicion of any "original" or "authentic" texts or writings—one will find it hard to accept his hypothesis. Still, if one suspends the question of authorship for a moment, one can at least agree with Guo Yi that the bamboo texts are quite likely an early version of the later "complete" *Daodejing* as it is found in the Mawangdui manuscripts and in the *textus receptus*, in their respective forms. Thus it is certainly highly plausible that the bamboo texts represent one source (or, more precisely, three sources), among others, for the later *Daodejing*. But even if one is willing to grant this, it is still not discernable which materials are older and more "original": those contained in the bamboo texts or those not contained in them. If one believes that the *Daodejing* is a collage of the materials of the bamboo texts with other materials, one still has no proof that these other materials are actually younger than the bamboo texts and mere additions. Why couldn't future excavations unearth older textual segments of the *Daodejing* that are not contained in the bamboo texts? Might not the bamboo texts actually contain younger materials that were then put together with older textual strata to comprise the now extant editions?

The bamboo texts of the *Laozi* contain textual segments that, in different forms and combinations, reappear in the later *Daodejing* either as chapters or as parts of chapters. They have obviously been included *en bloc* and were newly distributed within a larger whole. This internal changeability and the compatibility with other materials could, rather, as I believe, indicate that neither the bamboo texts nor the *Daodejing* that was later formed by integrating them were "complete" and "original" texts by any author. If the bamboo texts could be included, seamlessly and without being noticed by later editors, into another body of texts, why should they not themselves be constituted by various materials? Can't the fact that, before the discoveries at Guodian, neither modern sinologists nor traditional Chinese commentators or editors ever guessed that the materials found in the bamboo texts constituted an independent segment within the *Daodejing* lead one to the conclusion that the bamboo texts themselves could have been likewise seamlessly collated by using various sources that, today, we cannot tell apart from each other?

Unlike the two Mawangdui manuscripts, which present more or less the same text in different versions,[9] the bamboo texts consist of three sets of materials that do not coincide with each other (with the above mentioned exception of the final part of chapter 64). This heterogeneity of the bamboo texts, as distinct from the homogeneity of the Mawangdui silk texts, can be interpreted as another indicator of the heterogeneity of the *Daodejing* in the early stages of its development. Another indicator supporting the hypothesis that the *Daodejing* was put together from materials that were semantically and philosophically similar, but originally separate from each other, is the fact that the three sets of the bamboo texts were discovered side by side, but not in one piece. At the beginning of the second century BCE the *Daodejing* seemingly existed, regarding its contents, within the frame of its present-day form, but a century earlier, at the time of the bamboo manuscripts, the process that lead to such a specific frame,

---

9. Michael Friedrich argues for a strict separation of the two versions of the Mawangdui silk manuscripts of the *Laozi* in Friedrich, "Datierung."

was, apparently, not yet complete. However, even at this earlier stage certain chapters are, either as a whole or in part, already in a form that would then persist for millennia. Thus it may be concluded that even the bamboo texts do not present the "ultimate" raw materials of the *Daodejing*—if these should be identifiable at all.

Essentially, the bamboo texts can well be viewed, in my opinion, as evidence for the hypothesis that the *Daodejing* is a sort of anthology of philosophical sayings from the Warring States period that can be traced back neither to a single author nor to a group of specific authors. This hypothesis has already been formulated by D. C. Lau in such a convincing manner that even the discovery of the bamboo texts does not necessitate any fundamental changes to it.[10] I agree with Lau that the *Daodejing* consists of orally transmitted sayings, and consequently the bamboo texts from Guodian can be looked upon as documenting early written fixations of several materials that later became the *Laozi*. The bamboo texts of the *Laozi* obviously represent a stage in its textual history at which semantically congruent philosophical sayings had been collected and assembled into units. These units, that is, the later chapters, were then further expanded, regrouped, and joined with other materials of indeterminate age. The units, however, remained basically intact. This is at least one way to integrate the bamboo texts of the *Laozi* found at Guodian into a general history of this text.

If one is to accept such a view of the textual history of the *Laozi*, one can ask which elements of the text were more or less stable throughout the continuous modifications of the whole—and which were not. Particularly those elements that are tied to its oral transmission seem to have remained relatively unaltered: rhymes and rhythm, and the combination of lines into verses, stanzas, and chapters. Once several verses were amalgamated to form a textual unit or a chapter, they were unlikely to be taken apart again—but they could be expanded by the addition of other segments. Compared to the oral elements, the scriptural characteristics are highly unstable. The sequence of chapters is not fixed in the early stages of the text. The individual characters are written differently in the different manuscripts (and even within one set of materials such as the bamboo texts), homophones and synonyms are used frequently, and, particularly, the use of grammatical

---

10. Cf. D. C. Lau, *Lao Tzu: Tao Te Ching* (Hong Kong: Chinese University of Hong Kong Press, 1982); particularly appendices 1 ("The Problem of Authorship") and 2 ("The Nature of the Work").

particles is not standardized. The final particle *ye* 也, for instance, is used much more frequently in the Mawangdui manuscripts than in the *textus receptus*; and if one compares the two versions of the final part of chapter 64 in texts A and C of the bamboo texts, *ye* is used on one occasion (in text C: *shengren wu wei gu wu bai ye* 聖人無為故無敗也) and not in the other (text A). All this seems to indicate that the *Laozi*, despite the instances in which it was written down, was still largely oral in nature. Today we only have the text in writing (the oral transmissions cannot be excavated) and we are used to philosophical texts being written rather than told, but this may have hermeneutically prejudiced our reception of the *Laozi* and, so far, prevented an adequate understanding of its oral origins.

If one analyzes the changes within the textual history of the *Laozi*, it becomes obvious that, semantically, the maxims and mottos (such as those related to the strategy of nonaction or the cultivation of the body) remained largely the same while individual words could be altered. The various texts are highly different from each other when it comes to textual details,[11] and the bamboo texts are no exception to this, as we will later see in the analysis of chapter 19. But despite manifold changes of meaning, including the total reversal of specific words or sentences, there is hardly any philosophical divergence from basic Daoist teachings (like the ones just mentioned) to be observed, either in the text as whole or in specific chapters.

The relative stability of the text as a whole in comparison with the many changes in detail shows that the language of the *Daodejing* is not subject to strict argumentative or logical rules. The semantic variation of a word or a sentence in different versions of the text does not effect severe changes with respect to the philosophical teaching as long as the stanza or the chapter remains intact as a unit. The variations in the different versions of the *Laozi* can thus be understood as resulting from a transmission that values the evocative and poetic qualities of the texts and its elements more highly than it values the logical stringency of the argument or the continuity of the single word. The fact that, in later stages of the textual history, different commentators such as Heshang Gong 河上公 and Wang Bi interpreted the text differently without generally justifying their respective readings by claiming to have access

---

11. In my German translation of the Mawangdui silk manuscripts of the *Laozi* I have attempted to point out the semantic differences from the *textus receptus* chapter by chapter. Cf. Moeller, *Laotse*.

to any "original" text further supports a textual understanding that does not follow the maxim *sola scriptura*. It is not possible to relate the different interpretations of the *Daodejing* that developed within the Daoist tradition back to philologically different approaches to individual words or sentences. In other words, the many and significant differences in the use of characters in the different versions of the *Daodejing* did not give rise to the philosophical debates or schisms within the Daoist tradition. Unlike in the Confucian tradition, there is no quarrel between different schools in Daoism that developed on the basis of different textual versions of the "classics."

While scriptures were, "theoretically," certainly highly venerated and conceived of as highly powerful in ancient China—and particularly in the Confucian tradition—the practical dealings with written texts, as evidenced by the different versions of the *Daodejing*, were still highly influenced by an oral culture. This, at least, is suggested by a comparison of the different versions of this text. The more oral characteristics remained relatively stable throughout its history whereas the more scriptural aspects were unstable. This, in turn, could be understood as demonstrating that within a literary culture like ancient China, which did not have an alphabetical script, oral components were still highly influential. Such a hypothesis, however, is highly speculative and would have to be supported by much broader evidence than a simple comparison of a few versions of the *Laozi*.

II.

In the following I will discuss some specific differences between the Guodian bamboo texts of the *Laozi*, the Mawangdui silk manuscripts, and the *textus receptus* by analyzing the variations of a single chapter, namely, the nineteenth. The methodological question may be raised why I concentrate only on these versions. Firstly, it is quite natural to compare the Guodian bamboo texts with the Mawangdui silk texts because these are the only extant ancient manuscripts.[12] Of course, it

---

12. A concise overview of the extant *Laozi* manuscripts (excluding the Guodian bamboo texts) is: William G. Boltz, "Lao tzu Tao te ching," in *Early Chinese Texts: A Bibliographical Guide*, ed. Michael Loewe (Berkeley: Society for the Study of Early China and the Institute of East Asian Studies, University of California, 1993), 269–92.

would make sense to also take into account other early editions and commentaries from the era of the *textus receptus*. But since this essay is limited in space and is not supposed to be more than a first approach to a philological evaluation of the bamboo texts of the *Laozi*, I will restrict myself to the *textus receptus* as a third element of the comparison. I have chosen this version because of its great historical importance.

There are two reasons why the nineteenth chapter is well suited to a concrete comparison between the three versions of the *Laozi* under discussion. Firstly, since this chapter appears quite differently in all three versions, it offers many possibilities for observing textual changes. Secondly, it is the first chapter in text A of the bamboo manuscripts and thus it has some sort of special status—which, however, should not be exaggerated—within this group of materials.

I will begin my comparison of the different versions of chapter 19 by analyzing the Wang Bi version, then I will switch to the Mawangdui silk manuscripts, and, finally I will take a look at the bamboo texts. Thus I proceed in reverse chronological order.

In the *textus receptus*,[13] chapter 19 appears in the following version, which I quote along with the commentary by Wang Bi (in italics) in the translation by Ariane Rump and Wing-tsit Chan:[14]

絕聖棄智，
　　民利百倍。
絕仁棄義，
　　民復孝慈。
絕巧棄利，
　　盜賊無有。
此三者以為文不足，
見素，抱樸，
少私，寡欲。

---

13. See the edition of different versions and commentaries by Shima Kunio, *Rōshi kōsei*, 90–91.

14. Ariane Rump and Wing-tsit Chan, *Commentary on the Lao Tzu by Wang Pi* (Honolulu: University of Hawaii Press: 1979), 58. Rump's and Chan's translation is, at least with respect to this chapter, more accurate than the one by Paul J. Lin, *A Translation of Lao-tzu's Tao Te Ching and Wang Pi's Commentary* (Ann Arbor: University of Michigan Center for Chinese Studies, 1977), 34.

聖智才之善也。仁義人之善也。巧利用之善也。而直云絕。
文甚不足。不令之有所屬，無以見其指。故曰此三者以為文
而未足。故令人有所屬。屬之於素樸寡欲。

Abandon sageliness and discard wisdom;
    Then the people will benefit a hundredfold.
Abandon humanity and discard righteousness;
    Then the people will return to filial piety and deep love.
Abandon skill and discard profit;
    Then there will be no thieves or robbers.

However, these three things are ornaments and are not
  adequate.
    Therefore let people hold on to these:

Manifest plainness, Embrace simplicity,
    Reduce selfishness, Have few desires.

Sageliness and wisdom are the benison in a talent. Humanity and righteousness are the benison in a human being. Skill and benefit are the benison in a function. And yet the text just says to abandon them. Ornaments are greatly inadequate. If people are not enabled to hold on to something, there is nothing by which they will perceive the fundamentals. Therefore it is said: "These three things are ornaments and are not adequate." Hence let the people hold on to something: hold on to plainness, simplicity, and having few desires.

The text of chapter 19 can easily be divided into three parts according to its stylistic characteristics, its parallelisms, rhyme, and rhythm. This division is, and this is equally obvious, also semantic. The first three parallel verses admonish the Daoist ruler to suppress Confucian virtues and thus, by way of simplicity and plainness—so to speak, "naturally"—preserve the "innocence" of the people and the state. In this way the chapter immediately connects, as many commentators and sinologists have remarked, with the preceding chapters 17 and 18.

    The second part of the text is more problematic than the two others. Even though Wang Bi's commentary—as is by no means unusual for an ancient Chinese commentator—consists largely of paraphrases, it still gives reason enough for understanding the middle part in exactly the way as documented by Rump's and Chan's translation. "These three things" are obviously the three conceptual pairs in the first part that designate famous Confucian virtues which the Daoist sage ruler is supposed to abandon. Read along with Wang Bi, these three pairs of virtues are labeled "ornaments" (*wen* 文) in the second part of the chapter, indicating that they are depreciated as merely external adornments which, on their own, are worthless. The term *wen* is thus implicitly understood in the sense of a specific Confucian usage that, with respect to the *Lunyu* 論語, juxtaposes *wen* (external cultivation) with *zhi* 質 (inner quality) and thereby suggests that one without the other is insufficient. Furthermore, Wang Bi interprets the second part of the chapter in such a way that the Daoist sage, given the insufficiency of the Confucian values, has to supply the people with other values for their moral orientation. The Daoist virtues that should replace the abandoned Confucian ones are introduced very concisely in the third section of the text: plainness, simplicity, no selfishness, few desires.

This reading of the *textus receptus* along the lines of Wang Bi's commentary is accepted as the "standard interpretation" by many commentators and translators, even though there may be disagreements with respect to details. The silk manuscripts of Mawangdui, however, have led several commentators and translators to propose an alternative reading of chapter 19. The Mawangdui texts differ among themselves as well as from the *textus receptus* in regard to several individual characters, but I will not discuss these differences here, and, as far as I can see, other commentators and translators have mostly ignored them as well. Text B of the Mawangdui manuscripts inserts an *er* 而 ("and") between the first two phrases and before the last two characters. This too, I do not regard as an important variation. The third part of the chapter is only fragmentarily preserved in text A, but, with the exception of one character, completely preserved in text B. Here, there are no remarkable differences from the *textus receptus*. Thus, only the middle part remains available for constructing a different reading from the standard version. This is how the middle part appears in both Mawangdui texts:[15]

---

15. Text A adds a punctuation mark at the end of the second line. Cf. the Chinese edition of the Mawangdui silk manuscripts *Mawangdui Han mu boshu* 馬王堆漢墓 帛書, vol. 1 (Beijing: Wenwu, 1980).

此三言也，
　　以為文未足
　　故令之有所屬。

I originally interpreted this in my German translation[16] of the silk manuscripts in the following way:

These three sayings:
　　They are not yet sufficient for forming a pattern,
　　thus they shall be connected with something.

The essential difference between the silk manuscripts and the *textus receptus* is that instead of "these three things" (*ci san zhe* 此三者), here "these three *sayings*" are explicitly addressed (*ci san yan* 此三言). Although this variation was already known through the *Xiang'er* version of the *Laozi*, it had been given little serious consideration.[17] The characters *zhe* 者 and *yan* 言 can easily be mistaken for one another when written by hand, which may account for the difference between the two versions. In any case, the explicit mentioning of *yan* ("sayings") makes it impossible to read the Mawangdui manuscripts in the way of Wang Bi. The "three sayings" can hardly designate the previously mentioned six (three times two) virtues which the Daoist ruler is supposed to abandon. It seems much more plausible that the expression "these three sayings" designates the three sentences of the first part of the chapter.[18]

If one relates the first line of the middle part not to the more or less Confucian virtues, but, "formally," to the three sentences of the first part, then the term *wen* has to be understood differently. The three sentences can hardly be understood as external "ornaments." It is, instead, now possible to interpret the word *wen* here as "text" or (scriptural) "pattern." That the first three sentences on their own do *not yet* (*wei* 未) form a *wen* is what the silk manuscripts

---

16. See Moeller, *Laotse*, 190.

17. Cf. Shima Kunio, *Rōshi kōsei*, 90.

18. The additional difference from the *textus receptus*, the *ye* which follows the phrase *ci san yan*, can hardly be regarded as very important since this final particle occurs with such a higher frequency throughout the Mawangdui manuscripts. In this instance it does not change, in my view, the text grammatically or semantically.

state.[19] *As sentences* they do not yet sufficiently constitute a complete text, a poetical pattern. There is a lack that keeps them from being "formally" accepted as a completed poem of wisdom. More sentences are needed to round them off. "They," the "sayings" (as related to by the particle *zhi* 之 that appears in the second sentence of the middle part in the silk manuscripts and that replaces a grammatical object), have to be connected with more sayings.

Unlike the mainland Chinese commentators and translators of the Mawangdui manuscripts who tend to defy this textual evidence and hold on to the standard interpretation,[20] English translators dare to depart from the standard interpretation with respect to the middle part of this chapter. D. C. Lau writes:

> Concerning these three sayings,
>> It is thought that the text leaves yet something to be desired
>> And there should, therefore, be something to which it is attached.[21]

Robert G. Henricks writes:

> These three sayings—
>> Regarded as a text are not yet complete.
>> Thus, we must see to it that they have the following appended.[22]

---

19. This variation is also known through other versions (see Shima Kunio, *Rōshi kōsei*, 90) and corresponds with the paraphrase in Wang Bi's commentary. This fact can be interpreted as supporting the hypothesis that Wang Bi's commentary was made with reference to a different "original" as the present-day *textus receptus*. Cf. Wagner, "Wang Bi," and Boltz, "*Lao tzu*."

20. See as a representative example Xu Kangsheng 許抗生, *Boshu Laozi zhu yi yu yanjiu* 帛書老子注譯與研究 (The *Laozi* silk manuscripts. Commentary, Translation, and Research) (Hangzhou: Renmin, 1982), 102–3.

21. D. C. Lau, *Lao Tzu*, 293. D.C. Lau translates the Wang Bi version as follows: "These three, being false adornments, are not enough. / And the people must have something to which they can attach themselves" (p. 27).

22. Robert G. Henricks, *Lao-Tzu: Tê-Tao Ching; A New Translation Based on the Recently Discovered Ma-Wang-Tui Texts* (New York: Ballantine, 1989), 71.

Such a reading of the middle part[23] also affects the reading of the final part. In order for the final part to actually assume a parallel poetic pattern in conjunction with the first three sentences, it has to also consist of three sentences. In between the first and the third part, the middle part would function as some sort of axis. An extension of the third part by the addition of one further sentence or line, namely the first one of the following chapter 20 (*jue xue wu you* 絕學無憂, "Abandon learning, have no worries"), was considered by many commentators and translators even before the excavations at Mawangdui. This is because the first sentence of chapter 20 fits, both with respect to its contents and style, to the pattern of the last two sentences of chapter 19 and even connects lexically to the first part of that chapter. The Mawangdui manuscripts thus seem to prove that this line in fact "originally" belonged to chapter 19. Robert G. Henricks says the following about this issue in his translation of the silk manuscripts:

> Commentators and translators have gone back and forth on the issue of whether or not the first line of chapter 20 ("Eliminate learning and have no concern") is in fact the last line of chapter 19. I think it is. The lack of punctuation in the Mawangdui texts adds support for this cause. Moreover, it has always been clear that this line rhymes with lines 10 and 11 in chapter 19. . . . Finally, if the "text" has "three sayings," then there should be three appended lines as well.[24]

I myself thought so as well. But the bamboo texts do not support this hypothesis. There, the first sentence of chapter 20 does not seamlessly connect to the last one of chapter 19 as it does in the Mawangdui manuscripts, but is rather contained in the midst of text B, whereas chapter 19, as mentioned above, marks the beginning of text A. Thus it is clear that, at least for this version of the *Laozi*, the interpretation that was, among others, suggested by Henricks and myself for the Mawangdui manuscripts is out of the question. But this does not

---

23. Of the English translators of the Mawangdui *Laozi*, it is only Victor H. Mair who decides on some sort of middle way between the standard interpretation and the reading suggested by the silk manuscripts. He writes: "These three statements / are inadequate as a civilizing doctrine; / Therefore, / Let something be added to them." Mair, *Tao te Ching: The Classic Book of Integrity and the Way* (New York: Quality Paperback Book Club, 1998), 81.

24. Robert G. Henricks, *Ma-Wang-Tui*, 224. (Transcription modified.)

necessarily indicate that the bamboo texts anticipate the version of the *textus receptus*. In fact, the text of chapter 19 in the bamboo version is very different from both the *textus receptus* and the Mawangdui manuscripts. Particularly, the difficult middle part is here found in a different and hitherto unknown form.

The editors of the bamboo texts of Guodian transcribe chapter 19 of the *Laozi* in the following way:[25]

絕聖棄辯，
　　民利百倍。
絕巧棄利，
　　盜賊亡有。
絕偽棄慮，
　　民復孝慈。
三言以為辨不足，
　　或令之或乎屬
視素抱樸，
少私寡欲。

Two variations in this first part of chapter 19 of the bamboo texts are particularly interesting. Firstly, it is to be noted that the lines corresponding to the second and third verses in the *textus receptus* and the Mawangdui manuscripts are reversed. Secondly, instead of the clearly Confucian vocabulary, the bamboo texts use much more "neutral" terms. Instead of "sageliness" (*sheng* 聖) and "knowledge" (*zhi* 智 and *zhi* 知 in the Mawangdui texts and other later versions), "wisdom" (*zhi* 知) and "debating" (*bian* 辯) are to be abolished, and instead of the two Confucian cardinal virtues "humanity" (*ren* 仁) and "righteousness" (*yi* 義), "falsity" (*wei* 偽) and "insidiousness" (慮)[26] are to be abandoned. It seems that this part of the text only later took on its anti-Confucian tone by an exchange of the above terms.[27] There is only a marginal variation in the third part of the text: Instead of

---

25. Here, I do not cite the reconstructed text that contains a number of older forms of characters. Cf. *Guodian Chu mu zhujian*, 111.

26. The editors of the bamboo texts interpret this character as being homophonic and thus synonymous with *zha* 詐. Cf. *Guodian Chu mu zhujian*, 113n3.

27. Cf. Guo Yi, "Guodian," 51.

the character *jian* 見 ("to show"), which is found in the Mawangdui texts and the *textus receptus*, the bamboo texts have the character *shi* 視, which is likely used synonymously.

In the bamboo texts, the middle part of chapter 19 is significantly different from later versions. Firstly, like the Mawangdui texts, the bamboo texts speak of "three sayings" and not just "the three (things)." Then, however, instead of the problematic *wen*, there is a character which is reconstructed by the Chinese editors as 叟 and then transcribed as *bian* 辨. (Given its graphic similarity to the character used in the bamboo texts, the character *wen* could have resulted from a later copying error.) The second sentence of the middle part in the bamboo texts is entirely different from all later versions. Instead of the word *gu* 故 in the beginning, there is a *huo* 或, and the same character is then used once more instead of *you* 有. Instead of the expression *suo shu* 所 屬, there is the expression *hu shu* 乎屬. The occurrence of the character *zhi* 之 was already known through the Mawangdui manuscripts.

The middle part in the bamboo texts is hard to interpret. I would like to make the following suggestion: Unlike the Chinese editors who transcribed the character 叟 here as *bian*, one could perhaps understand it as a variant of *shi* 使—just as the Chinese editors transcribe the same character in chapter 55 in text A of the bamboo texts.[28] Moreover, in the second sentence one could follow the editors in interpreting the character *hu* 乎 as *hu* 呼 in the sense of "to proclaim," "to give an order." This would result in the following transcription of the middle part:

三言以為使不足，
　　或令之或乎屬

In line with a passage in the *Hanshu* 漢書,[29] the characters *ling* 令 and *shu* 屬 could be understood as being interconnected and meaning "commands and prohibitions." In this way, the two words would be semantically related to the word *shi* 使 (to give orders). Accordingly, a translation of chapter 19 of the *Laozi* as it appears in the Guodian bamboo texts could be:

---

28. Cf. *Guodian Chu mu zhujian*, 113.

29. Cf. the expression *shu ling zhou mi* 屬令周密 ("commands and prohibitions remained totally secret") in *Hanshu* (Beijing: Zhonghua, 1962), 3630.

Abandon wisdom and discard debating,
   and the people will benefit a hundredfold.
Abandon skill and discard profit,
   and there will be no thieves or robbers.
Abandon falsity and discard insidiousness,
   and the people will return to filial piety and care.

To turn these three sayings into orders is not sufficient,
   no matter if they are made commands or if they are
      proclaimed as prohibitions.

Manifest plainness, embrace simplicity,
   reduce selfishness, have less desires.

The whole chapter could thus be interpreted as reminding the regent that the proclamation of (in themselves appropriate) commands and prohibitions as they are introduced in the first part of the text is by no means sufficient for good government. More important for good government, in the Daoist fashion, is the self-cultivation and the self-restraint of the ruler. Only if he, as the third part of the text describes it, cultivates himself in a Daoist way and masters his body will he be able to master the people. Only in this way will he be able to make sure that the "benefit" mentioned in the first part will actually be achieved. Thus the ruler will not even need to coerce the people through commands and prohibitions, since they will, as one may conclude daoistically, find the proper way of living "self-so." In this way, chapter 19, standing at the beginning of the bamboo texts, would be an introduction to the two main Daoist issues which are so important in the Guodian bamboo texts of the *Laozi*: government by nonaction (and this also means not to work against a "natural" order by issuing "active" commands and prohibitions) and bodily cultivation (of the regent as a condition for order in society). Such an interpretation of chapter 19 in the bamboo texts is of course speculative, but it is also, I hope, not entirely implausible.

The change of the chapter 19 from the bamboo texts to the version in the Mawangdui manuscripts and then to the *textus receptus* is quite significant. A completely different meaning emerges in the Mawangdui texts as a result of the alternations in the chapter sequence and the different vocabulary. Perhaps, the scribes who produced the Mawangdui manuscripts have consciously put chapter 19 before chapter 20 because they believed, in line with their new interpretation of its meaning, that the first sentence of chapter 20 was actually the last of chapter 19. The second change from the Mawangdui texts to the *textus receptus* is not that radical, but still very conspicuous. Once more the text is semantically restructured and the interpretation provided in Wang Bi's commentary becomes the standard one. It is representative for the transformations of the text as a whole that the formal structure of chapter 19 (rhyme, rhythm, parallelism) remains relatively stable (if one does not take into account the specific issue of the last sentence—or the first of chapter 20) whereas, particularly, the written characters are subject to drastic changes. It is also remarkable that all three versions are distinctively and equally "Daoist" even though they all differ in meaning. No version violates the semantic frame of the *Laozi*. All three versions can therefore be understood as equally "authentic" Daoist writings. The earlier version cannot be singled out as more genuine than the others. In comparison with later versions such as the *textus receptus*, it is just more difficult to interpret the earlier versions because the historical context is largely unknown. The younger versions obviously document a philosophically and philologically more "developed" form of Daoism, whereas the earlier texts appear more like the "uncarved wood" into which later generations of Daoists chiseled increasingly exact and stable contours.

Index

Index

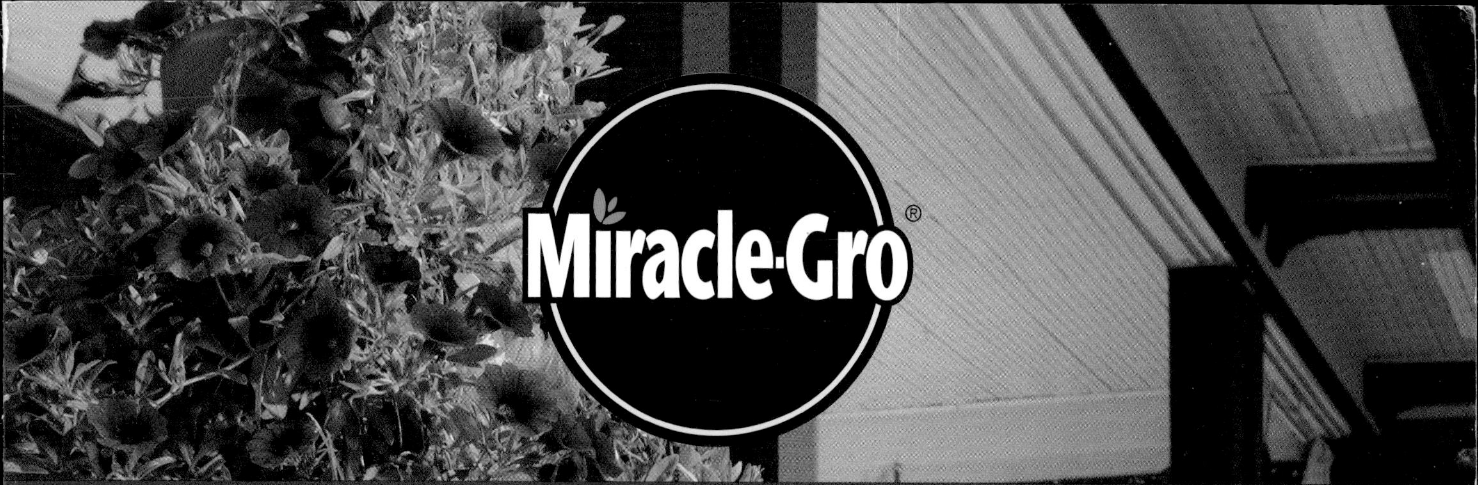

Beautiful GARDENS MADE EASY

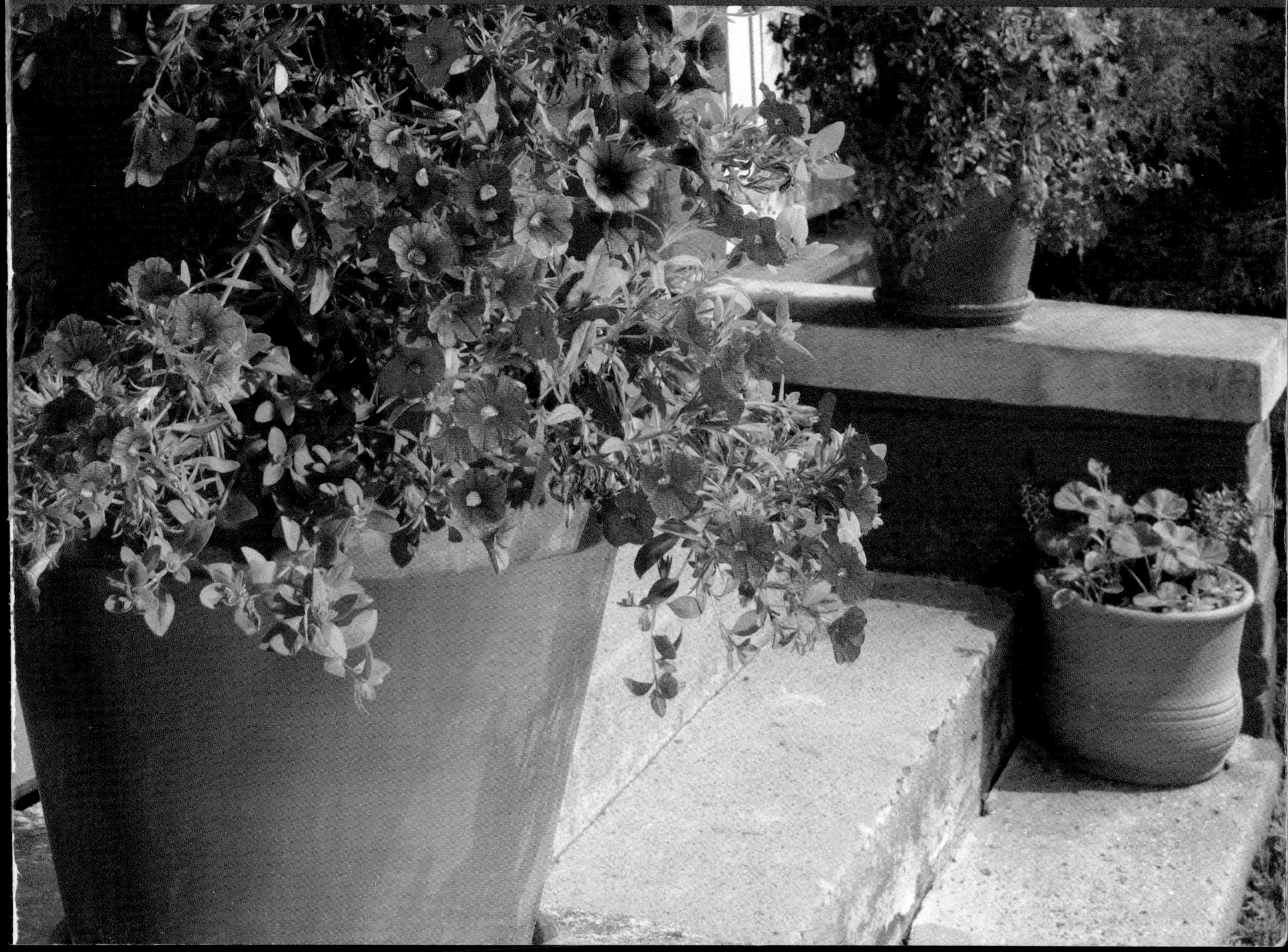

For more than 50 years Miracle-Gro has been the name America comes to for gardening success, and the reason is simple: We believe anyone can achieve joy, wonder, and satisfaction by the simple act of growing something and bringing beauty into the world. We're proud to bring you our first book, based on the vision that glorious gardens—and great gardeners—grow out of a series of small, easy projects. This book is full of beautiful ideas for every part of the yard and guides you to achieve them instantly and successfully. We hope you will discover more joy, wonder, and satisfaction in gardening each and every day.

Miracle·Gro®